SOUL FRIENDSHIP in the Celtic Tradition

ANCIENT INSIGHTS FOR TODAY

Copyright © Ray Simpson, 2021.

Anamchara Books
Vestal, New York 13850
www.AnamcharaBooks.com

Paperback ISBN: 978-1-62524-834-3
eBook ISBN: 978-1-62524-835-0

Scripture quotations labeled:

GNT are from the Good News Translation® (Today's English Version, Second Edition). Copyright © 1992 American Bible Society. All rights reserved.

KJV are from the King James Version of the Bible.

NASB are from the (NASB®) New American Standard Bible®, Copyright © 2020 by The Lockman Foundation. Used by permission. All rights reserved. www.lockman.org.

NIV are taken from the Holy Bible, New International Version®, NIV®. Copyright © 1973, 1978, 1984, 2011 by Biblica, Inc.™ Used by permission of Zondervan. All rights reserved worldwide. www.zondervan.com. The "NIV" and "New International Version" are trademarks registered in the United States Patent and Trademark Office by Biblica, Inc.™

NLT from the Holy Bible, New Living Translation, copyright © 1996, 2004, 2015 by Tyndale House Foundation. Used by permission of Tyndale House Publishers, Inc., Carol Stream, Illinois 60188. All rights reserved.

TLB are from The Living Bible copyright © 1971 by Tyndale House Foundation. Used by permission of Tyndale House Publishers Inc., Carol Stream, Illinois 60188. All rights reserved. The Living Bible, TLB, and the The Living Bible logo are registered trademarks of Tyndale House Publishers.

Soul Friendship in the Celtic Tradition

Ancient Insights for Today

RAY SIMPSON

I dedicate this book to those who,
through their friendship, their writings,
their challenge, their teaching, or their counsel,
have helped me move through painful struggles
toward my "place of resurrection."

Among these are:

STUART BURNS
ERIC HUTCHISON
FRANK LAKE
RUSS PARKER
SALLY SIMPSON

These people have also helped me
through their story or their writings:

Aidan

Brigid

Columba

Cuthbert

David of Wales

Frank Buchman

Francis de Sales

Brother Klaus

Thomas Merton

LEANNE PAYNE

BROTHER ROGER OF TAIZE

FATHER SERAPHIM

GILBERT SHAW

RUTH STAPLETON CARTER

THERESE OF LISIEUX

—Ray Simpson

www.raysimpson.org

Contents

Introduction 9

1. Rapport 13

2. Detachment 33

3. Envisioning 65

4. Discernment 95

5. Fostering 123

6. Faithfulness 149

7. Wildness 169

8. Prophecy 185

9. Fitness Training 199

10. Order 223

11. An Art 239

12. Dying 263

Introduction

The special friend who accompanies a person through life's journey is more precious than gold. Such a friend is one who experiences Divine wisdom and love as a constant resource—and is called to travel alongside and share all this with another.

The Irish of the early centuries of the Christian Era had a heartwarming name for this person: the Anamchara. *Anam* is the Gaelic word for soul; *chara* is the word for friend. *Anamchara* literally means "friend of the soul," and the soul in Celtic thinking, as in biblical language, refers to the total self. It does not refer to a piece of a person, the spiritual bit, as in Greek thinking, which split the spiritual from the material. Instead, "the soul" refers to the whole person—body, mind, and spirit.

The Anamchara was someone with whom a person could talk through practical matters, reveal hidden intimacies, and break through the barriers of convention and egotism to an eternal unity of soul. Celtic Soul Friendships were graced with affection. Soul Friends learned from each other, partaking of secrets so true that they reached places other friendships could never reach.

In this book, we shall use the term "Soul Friend" for what the Celts called the Anamchara, and we shall use the word "Seeker" to describe the person who invites a Soul Friend to help her discover her soul and her path. This book is written for people who are Soul Friends or who wonder if they might become one, and also for those who would like to have a Soul Friend and want to find out more about what this means.

Structure of This Book

Each chapter concludes with a summary of the lessons it contains, based on the wisdom of the past, followed by some exercises and suggestions for further reading. To be a Soul Friend, you must practice spiritual exercises yourself before advising others. To be a Seeker who invites someone to be your Soul Friend is to begin a journey yourself, an inner spiritual journey that requires you to leave behind ways that hold you back. Both Soul Friend and Seeker are on the journey, though the Soul Friend has been journeying longer or has been given grace to travel further. Therefore, the insights and exercises in this book will help everyone who has started out on the inner journey, including the general reader who has not yet found a Soul Friend to accompany him. What's more, the art of Soul Friendship is like a pyramid, and its base is in ordinary friendship—so some of the secrets and treasures of ordinary friendship are also woven into this book. Any of us can learn to be a better friend, and we can all learn to find the spiritual treasures hidden within any good friendship.

The ancient Celtic followers of Christ learned about Soul Friendship from the Bible, from their own cultural past, from the Desert Mothers and Fathers, and from their own experiences. Even now, hundreds of years later, they have much practical wisdom to share with us.

1

Rapport

Biblical Insights

It's no wonder that Soul Friendship was so important to the Celtic Christians: their minds and imaginations were soaked in the Bible, and the Bible teaches about friendship at its deepest level. The ancient Celts saw reality—both past and present, as well as spirit and matter—as a living whole. For them, the Scripture was alive; Bible characters were as real to them as the living members of their communities.

John, the Disciple of Christ: An Example of Soul Friendship

The Celts especially loved the Gospel of John, which portrays John and Jesus as Soul Friends. Although the word "anamchara" is not used, John is described as "the beloved disciple," and his relationship with Jesus was clearly intimate and deep. Celtic Christians regarded John as their spiritual father, and in the *Carmina Gadelica*, the prayers and poems of the Western Isles of Scotland collected in the nineteenth century by Alexander Carmichael, John is sometimes referred to as "John of love," "foster-son of Mary," and "foster-brother of Christ." These last two terms refer to the mother-son relationship Jesus brought about between his friend and his mother.

The fact that Jesus chose John as a Soul Friend should encourage us, because when they first met, John seemed rather unsuitable to enter into this relationship with God's Son. John was an ordinary fisherman. He was filled with ordinary selfishness and worldly perspectives: he and his brother James demanded "top places" when, as they expected, Jesus swept into power (Mark 10:35–45); and they wanted to curse a village that refused to welcome Jesus by calling down a violent thunderstorm upon it (Luke 9:54). Jesus nicknamed these tempestuous brothers "Sons of Thunder."

Jesus, however, could spot a person's potential. He knew that John's temper would mellow into tenderness. Jesus offered him unconditional love—and John responded to this love deeply and appropriately. From then on, John no longer thought of himself as a threatened, unwanted person, so he had no need to be angry. He knew himself now to be a beloved friend. As Jesus shared himself intimately with John, John became sensitive to the heartbeat of Jesus.

At the final Passover meal Jesus ate with his team the evening before his arrest, he told them he no longer regarded them as followers but as friends. As John leaned across him, Jesus confided in him. John and two others stayed with Jesus during three hours of terrible spiritual battle in the Garden of Gethsemane (Mark 14:33). Then, after more than two hours in agony nailed to a wooden cross, Jesus gasped out his dying wishes for the two people who were dearest to him: "Take John to be your son," he told his mother. Then he turned his gaze to John: "Take her to be your mother" (John 19:26–27). This moment became a part of our Christian heritage; people who wander into places of Christian worship often see portrayed on the altar the crucified Jesus with his mother and his adopted brother on either side of the cross. The outstretched arms of Jesus seem to say, "Come to me and you come also into my family."

> Jesus is both the model
> and the source of friendship.
> As the model of friendship,
> he calls the disciples
> to love as he has loved.
> As the source of friendship,
> he makes possible
> their own friendship
> through what he has given them.
>
> —GAIL R. O'DAY[1]

John's life continues to embody the spirit of Soul Friendship. Through Mary, John became Jesus' foster-brother to generations of believers. Tradition says that John suffered under the persecution of the Roman Emperor Domitian; he barely escaped being plunged in a cauldron of boiling water, and he suffered exile on the Isle of Patmos. John survived these trials and lived to old age at Ephesus, where (again according to tradition) he penned his three New Testament letters. Jerome records how, when John was dying, his friends asked him if he had any last message for them. "Little children, love one another," he said, as he had repeated in his letters. They asked him if that was all he had to say. "It is enough," he said, "for it is the Lord's command."

Love was the essence of John's friendship. In life, he became a spiritual father to many—a Soul Friend. Celtic Christians regarded John as their spiritual father, too. Eusebius, the third-century Christian historian, told a story that helps us see why Celtic Christians, who had passionate natures and compassionate Soul Friendships, drew such inspiration from John.

According to the story, John visited a Christian community near Ephesus, where he was especially drawn to one young man. John turned to the leader of the community and said, "I commit this young man into your care, and I call the whole community to witness that I have done so." The church leader took the young man into his household, discipled him, and baptized him. But afterward, the young man fell in with a gang of criminals and committed a crime. When the truth was discovered, he fled with the gang to the mountains, where he eventually became their leader. When John made a return visit to the community, he was upset to learn what had happened. He decided to go to the mountains and allow himself to be captured by these criminals so that he would be brought to the young man. When the young man saw John, he was so ashamed that he tried to run away from him. John was an old man by now, but despite his age, he ran after him. "My son," he cried, "are you running away from your father? I am old and frail—have pity on me! Do not let fear rule you, for I will stand for you before the Lord Christ. If need be, I will gladly die for you as he died for me. Stop, stay, trust! It is Christ who has sent me to you." John's appeal broke the young man's heart, and he threw away his weapons and wept. Side by side, as father and son, John and the young man came down the mountain. The man was restored to the church and to the Way of Christ.

Tradition also tells us that in his old age, John met with other church leaders to compile meditations on the life of Jesus that would help his followers advance along their journey of faith. In these pages (which we know as John's Gospel), he revealed intimate moments in Jesus' friendships. He records Jesus' friend Mary anointing his feet with costly perfume, and then drying them with her hair (John 12:3). John, more than any other Gospel writer, delights in the fragrance of intimacy expressed with all the senses.

For Jesus, friendship
is the ultimate relationship
with God and one another.

—GAIL R. O'DAY[2]

John recalls Jesus saying to his apostles, "I no longer call you servants, from now on I call you friends" (John 15: 15). Why? Because servants are not taken into the confidence of an employer—but friends are. Jesus had shared with those disciples everything his Father had told him. It is as if Jesus is saying to them, "Before I introduced a new way of friendship, your relationships were based on what you could get out of another person. From that old perspective, people were servants, customers, or clients. You related to them because of what they could provide, not because of who they were. I bring you a new way of relating, a new connection between you and others."

The quality of rapport we sense between biblical Soul Friends such as Jesus and John did not perish with them. The great Celtic saints Patrick and Brigid, according to the eighth-century *Book of the Angel,* shared "so great a friendship of charity that they were of one heart and one mind."

But today, we are an orphaned generation; we lack that deep sense of spiritual relationship. Women often seem to find it easier to make these intimate friendships, while men may have a harder time forming deep relationships with other men. Recent movements of God's Spirit have begun to rekindle these relationships among men. We all have much to learn from John.

The Trinity as the Source of Friendship

John helps us understand that the source of the love contained within Soul Friendship is the limitless Love of the Three Persons in God. John's writing portrays the Trinity as an eternal flow of friendship.

Friendship is the nature of God. God is one Love expressed as Three eternally loving Selves. "The Father loved me from before the world's beginning," said Jesus (John: 17:24); "the Helper will come—whom I will send to you from the Father . . . the Helper will give me glory" (John 15:26, 16:14). That is why Jesus laid down his life for us, because the Three Divine Selves had been eternally laying down their lives for one another. In his gospel, John presents the Creator as a Parent Friend (14:1–11), the Son as a woundable Friend (15:18–23), and the Holy Spirit as a helping friend (14:16–17). He uses the Greek word *parakletos* for the Holy Spirit, which means someone who comes alongside you, someone who is linked to you and who stands with you.

Jesus told his friends,
"I love you

just as the Father
loves me."

(JOHN 15:9)

Friendship Throughout the Bible

Examples of Soul Friendship have been recognized from early biblical times. Moses and Joshua, David and Jonathan, Ruth and Naomi, Barnabas and Saul, Paul and Timothy, and women such as Huldah (2 Kings 22:14) are all examples. The deep value of friendship is revealed throughout the Bible's wisdom literature.

In both Hebrew and Greek (the original languages in which the Bible was written), two common words for "friend" are related to words for "love." *Ahab* (Hebrew) means "loved one," and *philos* (Greek) means "dear one" or "loved one" (Acts 10:24, Galatians 6:1–2, James 5:16–20). The Greek word means "someone dearly loved (prized) in a personal, intimate way; a trusted confidant, held dear in a close bond of personal affection." The root word (*phil-*) conveys experiential affection; in other words, the Scripture's concept of friendship has to do with both love and experience, with the sort of love that is active. A friend is someone you appreciate and trust, someone to whom you commit yourself and with whom you share yourself. A friend is someone you want to do things for and give things to.

A faithful friend
is the medicine of life.

—ECCLESIASTICUS 6:16 KJV

Another aspect of Christ-like friendship is mutual giving and receiving. St. Paul urges Christians to "encourage one another and build each other up" (1 Thessalonians 5:11), "to bear one another's burdens" (Galatians 6:2), and "to admonish one another" (Romans 15:14). Soul Friendship in the Celtic style always has this same sense of mutual sharing between two people on a journey. Paul likens the Christian journey to a race run by an athlete (2 Timothy 2:5), and athletes understood then, as they do now, that they needed coaches. Perhaps Paul had Soul Friendship in mind when he referred to those who come to the aid of another (1 Corinthians 12:28).

The Wisdom of Friendship

The Bible makes clear that friendship needs to be "earthed" in wisdom; in other words, it must have deep roots to keep it sturdy and planted. Shallow friendships based on ego will not survive. The Book of Proverbs warns against depending on untrustworthy people when we are in trouble (25:19). The same book encourages us to actively cultivate wisdom, for it is not "an instant buy." In order to cultivate wisdom, we are encouraged to learn from mature people of experience and learning (13:20).

Follow Wisdom,
and keep to her ways
with all your heart.
Go looking for her,
and she will reveal herself to you.
. . .If you are willing to listen,
you will learn and become wise. . .
find someone who is wise,
and stay with him.
If you find someone
with understanding,
get up early to call on him;
wear out his doorstep
with your visits.

—SIRACH 6:26, 27, 33–36 GNT

Friendship Is Rooted in God's Love

At the beginning of the Bible, we read that God decided, "Now we will make human beings who will resemble us" (Genesis 1:26). Human beings are meant to resemble God by reflecting love. That is why, when Jesus was asked to select the greatest of the laws God had given to Moses, he selected these two from the Book of Deuteronomy: "Love the Lord your God with all your heart, with all your soul, with all your mind, and with all your strength," and, "Love your neighbor as yourself" (Mark 12:29–31, quoting Leviticus 19:18). In a reflection upon these words, John Goldingay wrote:

> You love God with mind, feelings and action . . . because that is what love involves. Our love is a reflection of God's, and God's is like that. God appreciates us, enjoys spending time with us, is glad to see us, finds us interesting, trusts us, makes a commitment to us, shares intimate secrets with us.[3]

All that applies to human relations. When you love another human being the same way you love yourself, this love, too, is a matter of mind, feelings, and action, just as God's love for us is and ours for God. Like love between God and us, love by its very essence must be two-way. It is unable to grow if only one of the two people wants that kind of friendship.

So why is it so hard to form these deep, committed friendships? Why do we often run away from them? The biggest reason is probably the risk: What if we give ourselves to another person and she doesn't give herself back? What if we end up being hurt? Another reason is that this level of friendship requires time and energy, both physical and emotional. We are naturally selfish beings, and we are often reluctant to be inconvenienced by others.

So what is the point of taking the risk and expending the energy? Why not hide from other people? One reason is the way our friends change us. As in marriage, which is a form of friendship if you are lucky, our friends create powerful forces in our lives.

Sometimes friends—and spouses—may decide they want to change us in particular ways. These changes may be good for us, and our friends may even succeed to some extent, but the change is likely to be external and shallow. We adapt our behaviors to avoid hassle, but we often don't change our hearts.

The more profound changes come about in friendship where people are not trying to force us to change. In this kind of relationship, your friend is committed to your well-being; she wants to do whatever she can to help you grow; but she leaves in God's hands the specific ways you grow.

In the meantime, she accepts you as you are. Perhaps you like and respect something about your friend. The more time you spend with her, the more you find yourself thinking the same way as she does. You may conclude that if the friend reckons a particular thing is important or interesting or worthwhile, there must be something in it. Your friend never asks you to change—but you end up changing your thinking, your attitudes, your life . . . all because of your friendship. Meanwhile, the same thing is going on in the other direction: your friends notice things about you that they admire. Or they may ask you why you act a certain way. This mutual regard between you and your friends encourages you to discover new things about yourself.

To love at all
is to be vulnerable.

—C. S. LEWIS[4]

Risk still exists. Our friends can hurt us. Intentionally or not, our friends often let us down. We also take risks as we share our secrets with each other—the risk of looking stupid and sinful and proud and narrow to the other person and thus to ourselves. But the risk is mutual. Both members of the relationship make the commitment to be vulnerable to the other.

God takes even greater risks when entrusting us with intimate secrets, sharing the ministry of the Godhead in the world with us, instead of the God-Self just getting on with it without our participation. And we take risks with God when we open up our lives to heavenly scrutiny and look at ourselves through God's eyes, when we commit ourselves to do what God wants.

Like our love for God, our love for someone else tends to develop gradually. The whole of God is not focused on us at once, and we do not give all of ourselves to God at once. This is normal and to be expected. Friendship, too, happens gradually. Both sides must stage by stage take ever-deeper risks, trusting more and more of themselves to the other.

Summary

Jesus had a deep rapport with God the Creator. As John matured, he developed a deep rapport with Jesus that was mutually strengthening, and as a result, John developed a deep rapport with the Trinity—Creator, Son, and Spirit. This is the basis of all friendship. We, too, can develop this rapport with God and with other human beings. To begin to do this is the foundation of being a good Soul Friend.

EXERCISES

The first three of these exercises relate to general friendship, while the last relates to Soul Friendship.

1. Slowly read John chapters 14 and 15. Repeat Jesus' words as if you were in his shoes. Allow the rapport that he had with his Father and with his friends to flow through you. Now review your relationships in the light of this meditation.

2. Focus your imagination on your favorite football team or music band. The best teams and bands have a rapport that flows out to their fans. Now think about your own life. What bits of your life flow out to others? To whom? What stops the flow? Visualize in prayer what would happen if nothing stopped the flow. Begin to live what you envisage.

3. Insecurity turned into love in the heart of the Apostle John. Reflect on places of insecurity within yourself, and bring these, one by one, to the unconditional love of Jesus.

4. Think of yourself as a Soul Friend relating to someone you know who might become a Seeker. Dedicate yourself to offer unconditional love as Jesus did to John. What might this mean for you?

Read More

The Gospel of John and the Epistles of John are the best places to start a deeper understanding of biblical Soul Friendship.

Listening for the Heartbeat of God: A Celtic Spirituality by Philip Newell (Paulist Press, 1997) will then help you gain a deeper understanding of John's meaning.

Notes

1. Gail R. O'Day. "I Have Called You Friends," Center for Christian Ethics at Baylor University, 2008, https://www.baylor.edu/content/services/document.php/61118.pdf.

2. Ibid.

3. John Goldingay. *St. John's Nottingham Newsletter*, December 1996.

4. C. S. Lewis. *The Four Loves* (New York, NY: Harcourt, Brace, Jovanovich, 1960), p. 169.

2

Detachment

Desert Insights

(the third to fifth centuries after Christ)

The practice of seeking out a specific experienced guide as a Soul Friend began in the fourth-century deserts. The Desert Mothers and Fathers practiced rigorous disciplines—so if you are a beginner, attempting these stringent practices would be like jumping in the deep end of a swimming pool when you are still learning to swim. Wading in from the shallow end is probably a better idea! You need not practice the desert disciplines unless you are ready.

In 313 CE, the Roman Emperor made Christianity a favored religion. Before this, being a Christian had been a sacrifice (one that could get you killed), but now it became a social advantage. Christians became attached to comfort, buildings, status, and the trappings of power. Often their faith became secondhand, their morals became lax, and their clergy became career-minded.

But some Christians were still hungry for God; they wanted to learn to live like Jesus. What were they to do? In the earlier centuries of Christianity, a few believers had already emigrated to the deserts of Egypt, Syria, or Palestine to live as hermits, basing their lives on the "beautiful attitudes" Jesus taught (Matthew 5:1–12). Now many more people joined them in the desert. These passionate believers realized that to advance in the true way of life, they had to be free of the distractions of their old life. They knew that time, space, and a Soul Friend were essential if they were to grow spiritually and be stripped of self-will.

A teacher ought to be a stranger
to the desire for domination,
vainglory, and pride . . .

> full of concern
> and a lover of souls.
>
> —AMMA THEODORA[1]

Imagine trekking all alone out into the Sahara Desert, finding a cave, setting up housekeeping there with only the most meager of supplies, and settling down to devote the rest of your life to prayer. This may seem like an extreme approach to the spiritual life—and yet the underlying dynamics are still with us. Individuals seeking a deeper reality become overwhelmed with modern life and seek out spiritual retreats. Some people in our society visit Buddhist monasteries in order to learn to overcome selfish desires and acquire inner well-being. Even people who are active in churches may realize they are carrying too much "baggage" to attend to the inner path. I have found this to be true in my own life; once when I was becoming too busy as a parish priest, my Soul Friend said to me, "Working on your inner life while carrying on an active life is like trying to repair an airplane while it is in flight."

So, although we may not want to adopt some of the more bizarre practices of those desert Christians (for we now know more about developmental processes that engender wholeness), we can nevertheless recognize the desert as an amazing laboratory from which we have much to learn. The Desert Mothers and Fathers have helped to shape generations of Christianity. Their example inspired the ancient Celts, even though they lived in different conditions; Celtic Christians found their own solitary places, which they named their "deserts." Today, many Christians are doing the same and creating "desert" days, weeks, or places of retreat.

The desert became a training ground of the spirit. Those who found it too difficult returned to the towns (and some coped by becoming seriously weird!). But many moved forward with God, and these became known as athletes of the Spirit. The older, wiser ones were called Abbas or Ammas; these were affectionate terms of respect, such as the words Poppa or Mama might convey. These were sought out as Soul Friends.

Let us each give
his heart to the other,
carrying the Cross of Christ.

—ABBA THEODORE[2]

The first desert Christians lived as hermits far from anyone else, but as the years passed, some lived near to others or formed communities. Although the lives of these desert Christians were anchored in solitude, this was not contrary to friendship. The cultivation of silence released a greater capacity for a friendship that did not depend upon trivia. John Cassian observed that the desert was pervaded by a deep spirit of friendship that was built on people being joined together in spirit rather than by being in one place. Cassian called this indissoluble bond the "common dwelling."[3]

News of these spiritual fathers and mothers stirred the imagination of sincere Christ-followers in the towns, and they too began to seek out Desert Fathers and Mothers as guides. Young people would test whether they might also be able to live this way by choosing an Amma or Abba to be their Soul Friend. They would share the work, the prayers, the silence, and the cell, and learn from the life as much as from the words of the older Christian. Soul Friends, at their very beginning, were cellmates. The word for Soul Friend in the Greek Orthodox Church—*syncellus*, "one who shares a cell"—still expresses this concept.

Busy townspeople made journeys to some wise old Desert Christian and ask him or her to be their Soul Friend for a weekend. Desert hermits paid visits to one another, and those with the clearest spiritual discernment would bring to light hindrances to spiritual growth that needed attention in others.

> When Abba Helle was staying
> with some brothers,
> they so trusted him
> that when he revealed
> the secret counsels of each of them,
> saying that one
> was troubled by fornication,
> another by vanity,
> another by self-indulgence,
> and another by anger,
> they could only respond,
> "Yes, what you say is true."[4]

Gradually, collections were made of the sayings of the Ammas and Abbas. Visitors to churches in the Celtic lands brought news of these Desert Fathers and Mothers for whom spiritual direction was part of the pursuit of holiness. For a time, John Cassian shared a desert cell with his friend Germanus in Bethlehem; later, the writings of Cassian and Athanasius about the Desert Mothers and Fathers were read in monastery libraries.[5] Eventually, the desert spirituality caught the imagination of Celtic Christians. They regarded the Desert Mothers and Fathers, with their single-minded passion for God, as spiritual superheroes.

The Hermits Paul and Antony

In the tenth century, Irish Christians often carved the figures of two of these great spiritual heroes, the desert hermits Paul and Antony, at the top of great stone crosses. After many solitary years in the desert, these two hermits had joined together as Soul Friends. The Celts loved the story of their friendship, which Jerome had recorded.[6]

For a hundred and thirteen years, the story went, Blessed Paul, the first known Christian hermit of the Egyptian desert, had lived the life of heaven upon earth. Meanwhile, in another part of the desert, lived Antony, an old man of ninety years. At first, Antony assumed that no better monk than he lived in that vast desert. As he lay quiet in his bed one night, however, he realized that there was, deep in the desert, another who was better by far than he. Antony knew he must make haste to find this spiritual giant.

Antony was a frail, old man, and he had no idea where he would find the other monk. But that didn't stop him, and he set out on his search. "I believe in my God," he said, "that he will show me his servant as he promised."

Antony followed the trail of a wolf that was seeking water by a cave. As he drew near the cave, he saw a light within. He called out, but Paul locked his door as soon as he heard his voice. Eventually, though, Antony's tears and entreaties convinced Paul that this visitor was a friend, not a foe. He opened wide the door, and the two men embraced and greeted one another by name.

"Look at me, the man you have searched for," said Paul, "and you look at a man who is soon to become dust."

Jerome records that despite their age and weakness, "for love's sake" they talked for a long time, speaking about the state of the world they had forsaken. As they talked, a crow flew into the cave with a large chunk of bread in its mouth; it perched in front of them and gently placed the bread before them. "At your coming, Christ has doubled his soldier's rations," Paul told Antony.

They understood this to be God's blessing on their meeting. Their friendship was something to celebrate, they realized. Together, they drank water from the spring, sang praises to God, and passed the night in vigil.

As the day dawned, Paul confided to Antony, "For a long time, brother, I have known that you lived in the desert. Long ago, God told me that you, my fellow-servant, would come to me. But since my time on earth has now come to an end, and since I desire that my body be dissolved so that I can be with Christ, it is clear that you have been sent in order to cover my body as it returns earth to Earth."

Antony wept at Paul's words. He could not bear the thought that this priceless friendship should be snatched from him so quickly. He pleaded that Paul would not leave him, but take him with him on his journey to heaven.

"You must not seek your own but another's good," Paul told him. "It is good for you to follow the Lamb of God, but it is good for the brothers who have come to live in the desert that they have you to model the life of Christ for them." Paul wanted to spare his friend the pain of seeing him die, so he added, "Go back to your cell and bring the cloak that Athanasius gave to you so that it can cover my dead body."

Amazement fell upon Antony, even in the midst of his grief, that Paul, who had lived in solitary silence all these years, could have known, no doubt through some inner revelation, of Athanasius, let alone of his gift to Antony of his cloak. Antony was so overcome that he could not answer Paul, for he saw and worshipped Christ within him. He silently kissed Paul's hands and his eyes, and then he set out on the five-day return journey to his cell.

This extraordinary once-in-a-lifetime Soul Friendship filled Antony with such awe that he didn't stop to speak even a word to his disciples at his cell, nor did he take time to gather food for the return journey. He was too eager to see his friend again, and he feared that his friend would have returned his spirit to God before Antony could return to him.

Antony's fears proved to be true. Before he reached Paul's cave, Antony saw a host of angels, companies of prophets and apostles, and Paul, climbing the steeps of heaven, shining white as snow.

The Relationship Between a Seeker and a Desert Soul Friend

This moment may have been Antony's peak experience of Soul Friendship, but it was not his first. One of the first things Antony did after his conversion was to go to a neighboring village and seek advice from an old man who had practiced the solitary life from his youth. Antony himself then became a Soul Friend to many.

Why was the relationship between an Abba or Amma and the disciple who came to learn the hermit life so fundamental? Jerome, who wrote much about these desert Christians, advised a friend not to set out into the unknown without a guide. To go into the desert without such direction would be foolhardy, for a person would be unlikely to survive the desert's ravages of body, mind, and spirit. Spiritual seekers needed teachers who could see into the hearts of the beginners and discern their appropriate courses. People had to learn the difference between running *away from* and running *toward* responsibilities; between rushing into false heroics and making steady progress in self-mastery; how to walk before they ran; and the difference between delusion and true revelation.

The novice's growth in the spiritual life was manifested primarily by the eagerness with which he renounced his own will and allowed himself to be guided. Two things were necessary if this relationship was to work: the Soul Friend had to teach by example as well as by verbal advice, and the Seeker had to be willing to obey without question. "Be an example, not a lawgiver," was a saying that circulated widely.

Cassian recorded this advice from Abba Moses:

> True discretion is impossible without humility. And the first proof of humility is to submit to the judgement of the seniors not only what we propose to do, but even what we think, so that by agreement with their decisions in everything we may know what is right and what is wrong. In this way, the young man will be taught to keep on the straight path and will be preserved from Satan's tricks and snares. For deception is impossible in the case of him who directs his life, not according to his own judgement, but according to that of his seniors. . . . The bad thought shrivels up the moment it is made public, and even before the senior has had time to pronounce his wise

verdict, the horrid serpent (dragged by confession into the light from his gloomy underground cave) scurries off as best he can and with a lively sense of confusion. In fact, his suggestions have the upper hand only as long as they are hidden in the heart.[7]

The cell was the first focus of the Desert Fathers and Mothers, as well as their disciples. The cell gave them the "soul space" in which wisdom and holiness could grow. And since being with a Desert Father or Mother in silence and solitude was more important even than listening to their words, sharing this soul space was a privilege the Soul Friend guarded and the Seeker cherished. The desert Christians believed that this soul space should be used both for silence and for opening up the heart to the other in a way that leads to peace and serenity. This mutual opening was known as *exagoreusis*, and the serenity it led to was known as *hesychia*.

Go to your cell
and your cell will
teach you everything.
—Abba Moses[8]

The second rule of the desert Ammas and Abbas was hospitality. Some cells had a window through which Seekers could receive advice at certain times. Other cells had two rooms, with space for a guest to sleep. And when younger people sought Abbas and Ammas as spiritual guides, they shared their lives with them: their cell, the silence, the prayer, the work, the meals—and occasionally, their conversation.

Detachment

The goal of both Soul Friendship and of the desert experience in general was to strip away all inessentials, so that only love remained. Physical comforts were left behind at the outset, but the emotional baggage every person carries was not so easy to set down. We all tend to hang on to pride, prejudice, and possessiveness for as long as we can, and this same baggage weighted down the desert hermits. In the busyness of urban life's society, we can hide these sins away from ourselves, but in the desert, they are exposed for what they are.

The collections of sayings and stories from the desert portray Soul Friendship within the framework of renunciation. The desert hermit gave up possessions, parents, sexual activity, and society. The Soul Friend (sometimes referred to as "the old man") encouraged his disciple's battle for spiritual freedom, while maintaining his own detachment. The

Soul Friend helped the Seeker recognize the things inside him that were substitutes for reality.

> As modern spiritual seekers, we may need to detach from:
>
> - resentment and negative attitudes
> - gossip
> - status
> - shopping
> - virtual reality
> - favoritism
> - possessions
> - possessive relationships
> - sexual compulsion
> - extreme busyness

The necessity of detachment was not unique to the Desert Mothers and Fathers; it was a theme common to classic Christian spirituality. In the desert, however, where people were freed from so many distractions, a spirit of detachment had a better chance to "take."

Modern Christians may dislike or disagree with the concept, because they think detachment will distance them from others. The ancient Celtic Christians, however, understood that detachment does not mean letting go of that which makes us human, but of that which prevents us from being *fully* human. We detach ourselves from anything that is not love—from possessiveness, from materialism, from selfishness—in order that love alone may reign in us. Detachment does not stifle spontaneity; instead, it sets us free to be like Adam and Eve who walked intimately with God in the garden, unashamed. When we lay aside the pattern of control by which we seek to cover up what is false in us, then what is true and beautiful can be revealed more clearly. What we love most deeply and that which really belongs to us come into their own. No one can take these from us.

Nor does detachment mean abdication of any true responsibility. It does not mean we skip off into the desert, leaving those we love behind to cope as best they can without us—but it does ask us to let go of the things we are not meant to waste our energy on. The following story from the Desert Fathers illustrates this.

A Seeker asked to join an Abba and use his spare cell. He told the old man that he wanted to renounce the world and become a monk.

"You cannot," the father told him.

"I can," the Seeker replied.

"If you want to do this, go and renounce the world and then come back here and sit in your cell," the old man told him.

The young man departed and gave away half of his money, keeping a hundred coins for himself, and returned to the monk.

"Go and sit in your cell," the old man advised.

While the Seeker was sitting there, his thoughts said to him, *That old door needs replacing.*

Later, when the Seeker mentioned this to the monk, the old man told him he had not renounced the world. "Go and do that, and then come back here."

The young man gave away ninety coins and hid ten for himself. On his return, he informed the old man, "Look, this time I have really renounced the world."

"Go and sit in your cell," said the older man.

As the young man sat there, his thoughts said to him, *The roof is old and wants replacing.*

In due course, he told the old man what his thoughts were saying. "Go away and renounce the world," the old man told him.

The young man went away again, gave away his last ten coins, and returned. Again he sat in his cell. This time his thoughts said to him, *Everything here is old, and a lion is coming to eat me up.*

When he told these thoughts to the old man, the old man nodded. "I expect everything to come down on top of me, and the lion to come and eat me up. There is nothing I can do about it. Now that you have renounced the world, go, sit in your cell, and pray to God."

The Spiritual Battleground

For the Desert Mothers and Fathers, the human heart was the most important battleground. There, positive qualities (the virtues) battled destructive qualities (the passions).

THE PASSIONS

When the Abbas and Ammas spoke of "passions," they were not referring to strong feelings, for they certainly believed in being passionate for good. Instead, "passions" were drives that were destructive and enslaving. This desert concept still offers us a useful tool we can use to increase our ability to love.

To be made in God's image means to see all people and things as they truly are, as God sees them, through the lens of love. If we follow this line of thought, to truly love we must be able to see God, others, and even ourselves as more than extensions of our own needs. The world around us is not there simply to satisfy our selfish urges—but the passions obscure this way of seeing in love. They also rob us of the freedom to make real choices and act on them. The fear of abandonment and the compulsive need for approval that many of us carry over from childhood steal our ability to choose the way of love.

A fourth-century monastic teacher, Evagrius Ponticus, regarded anger as "the most fierce passion," and describes it as "a boiling and stirring up of wrath"[9] against someone who has given injury—or is thought to have done so. Anger constantly irritates the soul, and above all at the time of prayer, it seizes the mind and flashes the picture of the offensive person before our eyes. The angry person is not responsible for the origins of her anger, but can nevertheless choose to nurse that anger to the point where it controls her—"for both anger and hatred increase"—or she can fight against it and refuse to let it reach the point of becoming destructive.

> Evagrius Ponticus warned people
> about these eight passions:
>
> - gluttony (that is, never being satisfied with what we have)
> - lust for other people's bodily parts
> - acquisitiveness (wanting things)
> - depression
> - anger
> - restless boredom
> - love of flattery
> - pride

All the desert guides believed these passions must be wrestled against and mastered. Father Ammonas told someone he had spent fourteen years in Scetis asking God night and day to give him the victory over anger.[10] Tools that were commonly used to tackle these passions were fasting, silence, and abstinence from sleep, sex, and ownership.

THE VIRTUES

Detachment and wrestling against the passions were not ends in themselves, however. Instead, for the Desert Mothers and

Fathers, these were merely the preconditions for the flowering of "the virtues." The virtues were the opposite qualities of the destructive passions; they included self-control, chastity, generosity, gentleness, peaceableness, contentment, appreciativeness, and humility. Father Dorotheus taught that we are made in God's image, so God has sown the virtues like seeds within us. We are called to resemble God, as Jesus taught: "Be merciful for your Father is merciful" (Luke 6:36).

One of the Fathers taught that three particular virtues should be honored: the fellowship of Holy Communion, the fellowship of a shared meal, and the washing of another person's feet. Antony taught people to make a conscious pursuit of one virtue at a time.

"Virtue," taught one Desert Father, "leads to God and unites us with one another."[11]

After monasteries came into being, Antony wrote letters to the monks to help them grow in the virtues. "I, as your elder, will share what I know and the fruits of my experience" he wrote.[12] In his first letter he described how the human body from top to bottom—the tongue, the hands, the belly, the genitals, the feet—could be integrated into God's love. He repeated to his disciples that his love for them was not limited to the body but was also of the spirit.

Antony soon realized that even many desert Christians had no idea of the different kinds of will that humans express in their lives. He urged them to distinguish between these three: God's all-perfect and saving will; our own human will, which, even if it is not destructive, is not saving; and the devil's will which is wholly destructive. He might have added a fourth will for town-dwellers: the will that other people lay upon us.

> Whoever hammers a lump of iron
> first decides what
> he is going to make of it,
> a scythe, a sword or an axe.
> Even so we ought
> to make up our minds
> what sort of virtue
> we want to forge
> or we labour in vain.
>
> —ANTONY[13]

Entering a Personal Desert with a Soul Friend

Without a desert environment—an "empty space" of some form—we are unlikely to get to know either ourselves or God. We will find it hard to absorb "the wisdom of the desert." Without purity of heart—undiluted commitment to our journey with God—spiritual direction is a waste of time. And without a willingness to get to know every part of ourselves, including our earthy physical parts and our disguised qualities, we cannot enter into the reality that is God's will for us.

Yet it is no light matter to enter any form of desert. A physical desert has no water, trees, or obvious beauty; nor does an inner desert. You cannot truly enter an inner desert if you are trying to fit it into your life around other things—or if you are trying to fit other things into the desert. To enter a desert you have to leave behind other things. And you have to be prepared for things to get worse before they get better.

In the desert
our spirit travels blindly
in directions that seem
to lead away from vision,

away from God, away from
all fulfillment and joy.

—THOMAS MERTON[14]

Most of us are attached to things that prevent us from journeying to the place where there is nothing. Some of us attach ourselves to superficial or self-flattering talk in order to hide from a feeling that our inner cores are hollow. If that's the case, we need to detach from these false defenses and walk into the desert, accompanied only by the honest pain of confronting our own reality. Meanwhile, the role of a Soul Friend would be to give us space and gentle encouragement to get in touch with these feelings—and then to discuss how we can have a dialogue with God about our inner defenses. The Soul Friend is with us as we journey, but she should not play God by giving us superficial palliatives. Her role is not to make us feel better but to help us grow. She needs to beware of sidetracks that might distract us from the challenge of the desert experience.

Others of us may fear that our center is a seething, out-of-control mass, so we button up everything by successfully organizing others and ourselves. Those of us who are like this may not allow ourselves to have a Soul Friend at all, but if we do, we will want the Soul Friend to provide us with a list of tasks we can accomplish and tick off as achievements. A Soul Friend may, at first, use this approach, but he should always steer our attention away from the external world toward the inner life. For example, the task could be to pay attention to the times during the day when the stomach is most taut, and to note the things that triggered this. Then, when the Soul Friend and the Seeker next meet, they might discuss the feelings that accompanied this. Gradually, the Seeker will enter a desert place where he learns to explore his body and feelings. In the process, he will finally allow his vulnerability to come to the surface.

A third type of person may despair of sustaining a true relationship. Those of us who have these feelings often wrap a cocoon around ourselves, so we can avoid interacting with others. We may pour our emotions into idealizing the future or the past, in order to avoid the disharmony of the present. If we have this set of defenses, we need to detach from them and acknowledge our raw emotions. As we venture into our desert experience, our Soul Friend will need to confront us with the here and now.[15]

You do not go to the desert
to find identity,
but to lose it,

> to lose your personality,
> to be anonymous.
> You make yourself void.
> You become silence.
> You become more silent
> than the silence around you.
> And then something
> extraordinary happens:
> you hear silence speak.
>
> —EDMOND JABES[16]

Sometimes, however, we enter a desert experience unintentionally. When that happens, we may feel we have come to a standstill in our spiritual journey. We assume this is a failure on our part, and we want our Soul Friend to suggest ways we can move on. The Soul Friend will need to find out if this standstill is caused by willful refusal to heed inner promptings. If it is not, the Soul Friend needs to say, "Do not run away from this darkness. Do not torture yourself. Keep still, open, trusting in One who is present even here with you. Something will emerge from this time of arid darkness."

Spiritual direction in the Soul Friend tradition does not beat about the bush! The starting point is always to surrender to God's will. As you allow yourself to enter the desert, something will seep into your soul that is deeper than the darkness, something beyond definition. You will be purified. The outer self, the ego that depends on the senses, may be restless and unsatisfied, but the deeper core of the true self will rest in the will of God.

Summary

The hermits Paul and Antony discovered Soul Friendship in the desert. When many Christians followed after them, the whole desert was pervaded with a spirit of friendship. One method of a desert Soul Friend was to share his cell with a Seeker for a short or long period. The purpose of this discipline was, through ceaseless prayer, to strip away negative, self-centered habits, so that God's qualities—such as patience, gentleness, and love—could flower within.

EXERCISES

1. Whether you are a Soul Friend or a Seeker, make a list of the negative passions that hijack true love in your life. Number them in order, according to the strength of their hold over you—and then decide what tool you will use to combat the "passion" at the top of your list.

2. Whether you are a Soul Friend or a Seeker, make four lists of specific examples of the four types of will (God's, yours, others', evil) that currently seek to control your life.

3. Whether you are a Soul Friend or a Seeker, make a list of the virtues you most desire, and number them in order of priority. Decide what steps you will take to practice the number-one virtue.

4. Imagine you are Soul Friend to a Seeker who can only see you once a year after a long journey. How will you arrange your house, your schedule, your heart, and your mind so that the Seeker experiences *exagoreusis* and *hesychia*?

Read More

The Desert Fathers: Sayings of the Early Christian Monks translated by Sister Benedicta Ward of the Fairacres Community (Penguin, 2003) contains a selection of the sayings of the Desert Fathers.

Wisdom of the Desert Fathers and Mothers: Ancient Advice for the Modern World by Philip Bochanski (TAN Books, 2020) is another good source.

Notes

1. Mary Forman. *Praying with the Desert Mothers* (Collegeville, MN: Liturgical Press, 2005), p. 17.

2. Armand Veilleux, trans. *Instructions, Letters, and Other Writings of Saint Pachomius and His Disciples* (Kalamazoo, MI: Cistercian Publications, 1982), p. 107.

3. Philip Schaff, ed. *Nicene and Post-Nicene Fathers* (New York, NY: Cosimo, 2007), p. 206.

4. Quoted in Edward C. Sellner's *The Celtic Soul Friend* (Notre Dame, IN: Ave Maria Press, 2002), p. 79.

5. The sayings, anecdotes, and short stories of the fourth-century Desert Fathers and Mothers were handed down and collected in the fifth century. One collection was arranged alphabetically under the name of a monk; another collection was arranged under themes. In addition, groups of monks

would preserve the sayings of their founders. These were also collected together and published in Latin as *The Lives of the Fathers*. Other early writers such as Athanathius, Jerome, John Cassian, Evagrius, and St. John Climacus also wrote about some of the Desert Fathers and Mothers.

6. This story is based on an account in Jerome's *The Life of St. Paul: The First Hermit*. There is an English translation in Helen Waddell's *The Desert Fathers* (New York, NY: Vintage, 1998).

7. John Cassian. *The Conferences of John Cassian* (London, UK: Aeterna, 2000), ch. 11.

8. John Cassian. *Western Asceticism* (Whitefish, MT: Literary Licensing, 1952), p. 42.

9. Bernard McGinn and Patricia Ferris McGinn. *Early Christian Mystics: The Divine Vision of the Spiritual Masters* (Chestnut Ridge, NY: Crossroad, 2003), p. 49.

10. Bernadette McNary-Zak. *Useful Servanthood: A Study of Spiritual Formation in the Writings of Abba Ammonas* (Collegeville, MN: Liturgical Press, 2010), p. 35.

11. Benedicta Ward. *The Sayings of the Desert Fathers: The Alphabetical Collection* (Collegeville, MN: Liturgical Press, 1984), p. 78.

12. Robert C. Gregg, ed., trans. *The Life of Antony and the Letter to Marcellinus* (Mahwah, NJ: Paulist Press, 1980), p. 43.

13. Tim Vivian, ed. *Becoming Fire: Through the Year with the Desert Fathers* (Kalamazoo, MI: Cistercian Publications, 2008), p. 87.

14. Thomas Merton. *Seeds of Contemplation* (New York, NY: New Directions, 1949), p. 153.

15. These three examples correspond to Enneagram types 2, 3, and 4 (Helper, Achiever, and Individualist). The Enneagram is a method of classifying human beings into nine categories of personality, each having distinctive traits and defense mechanisms. Different personality types tend to put up particular barriers that prevent them from entering the spiritual desert where they will find reality. The Enneagram can be a useful spiritual tool during the process of Soul Friendship. A helpful book that explains the different types of personality the Enneagram can bring to light, the defenses each personality type tends to put up against spiritual reality, and how Soul Friends can work with them is *Enneagram Companions: Growing In Relationships and Spiritual Direction* by Suzanne Zuercher, O.S.B. (Notre Dame, IN: Ave Maria Press, 1971). The following books are some of the many others that also provide more information on the Enneagram: Don Richard Riso and Russ Hudson's *Understanding the Enneagram; The Practical Guide to Personality Types* (New York, NY: Houghton Mifflin, 2000); Helen Palmer's *The Enneagram in Love and Work: Understanding Your Intimate and Business Rela-*

tionships (New York, NY: HarperOne, 1996); and Claudio Naranjo's *Transformation Through Insight: Enneatypes in Life* (Chino Valley, AZ: Hohm Press, 1997).

16. Edward Jabes. *The Book of Margins* (Chicago, IL: University of Chicago Press, 1993), p. xvi.

3

Envisioning

Pre-Christian Insights into Soul Friendship

Tony Blair, who was Britain's prime minister at the turn of the millennium, had a spiritual mentor; members of Britain's royal family have spiritual directors; and Oprah Winfrey has chosen Rob Bell to be her spiritual mentor. These public figures are following in the footsteps of the Soul Friend tradition, for in the ancient Celtic world, rulers often turned to wise spiritual elders for direction and guidance. The elders' role in the kingdom was recognized and honored.

This was a pre-Christian tradition as well. The Druids helped build the foundation for what would later become the Christian concept of the Soul Friend. Of course, Christian Soul Friends discarded some of the pagan spiritual guides' methods, such as casting spells or conjuring up spirit powers that were not God-centered. At the same time, however, ancient Celtic Christianity recognized the value of the spiritual guide as someone who communicated vision to the people, someone who could pass on both the memory of the past and the wisdom of Nature.

Today, few Soul Friends are likely to have national leaders as their Seekers. Nevertheless, the ancient Druids' role reminds us of the power Soul Friends can have. The Soul Friend's vision can influence leaders and help shape entire communities. In today's world, more than ever, we need the power of a Soul Friend's vision. True friendship always releases the power of possibility.

Celtic Soul Friends drew their primary inspiration from the Gospels and from the Christian Fathers and Mothers of the Desert, but they also inherited from their pre-Christian society the tradition of envisioners: Druids, bards, and shamans. Local rulers employed and consulted Druids, and doubtless, others did too. When the great Celtic saints Patrick, Columba, and Brigid were young, they were taught by

Druids. Druids were the closest pagan equivalents to Soul Friends. They were holistic advisors to the community's leaders (while Soul Friends worked within the community as a whole). The Druids were steeped in the wisdom of Nature, folklore, and philosophy.

> The justice of the king
> consists in having
> a wise counselor.
>
> —SEVENTH-CENTURY CELTIC MAXIM

While the Druids were generally associated with a particular ruler and community, Celtic bards wandered from place to place, where they would be invited to speak or sing. These envisioners provided a "guidebook" to the past and the present, to the worlds of Nature and of the spirits. Their vision helped link the entire community—including the natural world and the spiritual world, as well as human society—in an all-embracing friendship.

The word *pagan* became a term of abuse during later centuries, synonymous with ungodly or unchristian, but its original meaning was simply "someone from the country."

Before Christianity came to Britain, the people we now call pagans were following the highest wisdom they knew, much of which they found in the world of Nature. Celtic pagan society valued people whose job was to raise people's sights, to inspire them to see a fuller, richer vision of reality.

Celtic Christians drew from this heritage; they sifted it and transformed it. Christianity introduced the Celts to a Person who was the Source of what was good, who changed what was bad in their society. They were secure enough in their faith not to feel threatened by others' viewpoints. They confronted them when necessary and learned from them when possible.

The Role of Druids, Bards, and Shapers

Some scholars believe the root of the word *druid* means "knowledge of the oak," while others think it means "those whose knowledge is great." It took twenty years of education to become a Druid; the entire body of folklore had to be committed to memory, since nothing was written—and because Druids passed on everything from memory and wrote nothing down, much of what we know about them comes from biased Roman writers who belittled them. Scholars argue as to the exact nature of their practices. Some allege that Druids once offered humans as sacrifices, but there is no evidence of this from sixth-century Britain. Julius Caesar recorded that Druids acted as arbiters in all private and public matters, as well as officiating at rituals and sacrifices; and Pliny described them as doctors as well as magicians. Saints Clement and Cyril of Alexandria saw Druids as enlightened philosophers who believed in the immortality of the soul.

Pomponius Mela (first century CE)
described the Druids as:

"teachers of wisdom,
who profess to know
the greatness and
shape of the earth
and the universe,
and the motion of the heavens
and of the stars and
what is the will of the gods. . . .
They teach many things
to the nobles of the race
in sequestered
and remote places."[1]

In ancient Ireland, the social system could be broken into three groups: the warriors, the farmers, and the craftspeople. This third small but influential group was known as the *aes dana*—the people of learning or poetry. They included poets, historians, lawyers, doctors, skilled craftspeople, the storytellers. Their moral authority was sometimes equal to that of the ruler, and they had the privilege of traveling anywhere as honored guests. They were the purveyors of the tribe's values, the advisors to its rulers, the communicators to the people.

The poets, or bards, were as influential in ancient Britain as they were in Ireland. Merlin, of the Arthurian legends, was originally the bard of King Gwenddlau. Taliesin was the bard of Urien, King of Rheged.

Celtic author Caitlin Matthews describes the work of the ancient bard Amergin:

> In Amergin's mystical identification with all things, he becomes one of the physicians of the soul, reweaving the scattered elements of life into a new wholeness. This is the task of the Celtic poet, whose skill is to bring the soul to the point of vision, rest, and stillness. The music of their healing skill is known by three strains: the laugh strain which raises the spirits; the sorrow strain, which causes the release of tears; and the sleep strain, which brings rest to troubled souls.[2]

A bard who was asked from whence he came, replied:

*I move along the columns of age,
along the streams of inspiration,
along the fair land of knowledge,
the bright country of the sun;
along the hidden land,
which by day the moon inhabits,
along the first beginnings of life.*[3]

Shape-shifters or shamans—people with extraordinary psychic connections to the natural world—also played a role in the ancient world of the Celts, as they do with many primitive peoples. Societies based on hunting and gathering needed someone to help them make sense of the mysterious natural world on which they depended for their livelihoods. Hunters wanted to protect themselves from the angry spirits of animals they had killed, and so the shaman emerged—a person who could clothe himself with parts of the animal, go into a trance or out of the body, and so gain a rapport with and an influence over the spirits of the natural world. Shamans could also act as clairvoyants to humans and could put spells upon people, either through hypnotism, drug potions, or channeling of psychic or spirit forces. The shaman was thought to be the lord of the animals and of the spirits.

In the stories of the pagan Celts, the heroes frequently changed their shapes and became birds or animals. Gwion, for example, turned into first a hare, then a fish, and then a dove to escape the witch Ceridwen. The harpers of Cain Bile turned themselves into deer to avoid being captured. When Llew was pursued by Blodeuwedd, he turned into an eagle.

Sometimes shamans were prophetic. When Fedlimid's pregnant wife issued a primal scream, Cathbad predicted that her child would be a tall, lovely, longhaired woman, but that she would also be a source of contention and slaughter.

As Amergin White Knee, chief bard
and shaman of the Milesian invaders,
greeted the land of Ireland from his ship,
he believed he could remember
many transmigrations:

> I am a stag of seven tines;
> I am a dewdrop let fall by the sun;
> I am the fierceness of boars;
> I am a hawk, my nest on a cliff;
> I am the salmon of wisdom.
> Who (but I) is both the tree
> and the lightning that strikes it?[4]

What Christians Rejected from the Pagan Guides

The prayer known as St. Patrick's Breastplate, which scholars believe to be from seventh- or eighth-century Ireland, pinpoints some key elements in the pagan heritage that Christian Celts rejected. Any link with demons, that is, spirits who are not aligned with Christ, was rejected. The casting of spells was rejected, and so was "knowledge unlawful." This probably refers to those who delved into the spirit world for ulterior motives. Any approach that lacks integrity is unacceptable. The test "by their fruits shall you know them" was applied. Anything that violated the spirit or body—anything that led off from the path of love—was unlawful.

This day I call upon
the might of Heaven
to protect me
from snares of the demons,
from evil enticements,
from failings of nature,
from one man or many,
that seek to destroy me
nearby or afar.
Against false prophesyings,
against knowledge unlawful
that injures the body,
that injures the spirit.

—FROM ST. PATRICK'S BREASTPLATE

What Celtic Christians Refashioned from the Pagan Guides

Celtic Christian leaders befriended many of the pagan envisioners, even as they gradually replaced them and took on some of their roles in a new way. They said, in effect, "We are grateful our society has people to envision deeper reality—but have you noticed how sometimes this goes wrong? Envisioners can build castles in the air that delude and come to nothing; they can use their power to inflate their own egos or gain control over others. Power often corrupts, and this is true of psychic power as much as physical power. Spiritual leaders should serve others, rather than manipulate them. Moreover, it is not always helpful for individuals to be told what will happen to them in the future. It is like taking someone into a minefield to dig for gold: yes, treasure may be found there, but while searching for it, the mines can explode and destroy the searcher. Nor is everything in the unseen world good; spirits can be deceitful and malevolent, and so we should only seek to enter the invisible realm through the Ruler of that world, whom we know as God's Son Jesus Christ. We admire and indeed emulate your well-honed intuition, but intuition can be wrong—and when it is right, it can be used for evil. It needs to be accountable to a higher Power, the High King of the universe."

Christianity introduced the pagan world to a vision of God as revealed through Christ. Many of the Celtic seers turned aside from ways that tuned them into spirits and psychic currents that were not Christ-centered. Their own vision and hearts needed to be purified, and so they prayed, "Be thou my vision, thou Lord of my heart." But they continued to shape their society; they did not leave the whole arena of envisioning behind to the pagans. Purified by penance and humbled by service to the poor, they allowed the Lord of seen and unseen powers to pour out Divine gifts of seeing and wisdom, poetry and shaping. Always these were tested by Scripture, and always their purpose was to build up souls for the glory of the High King of all creation.

> Where there is no vision
> the people perish.
>
> —PROVERBS 29:18 KJV

Over time, a new framework evolved, and pagan guides were replaced by Christian roles. More personal, God-centered relationships developed, but Christian Soul Friends often retained the envisioning role of the old guides. The Christian Anamcharas came to have a variety of roles: Some—such as Patrick, Brigid, and Columba—were healers, seers, and spiritual guides. Many—such as Aidan, Hilda, and David—were tutors both to younger students and to adults. Some were mystics like Samthan of Clonbroney and Maedoc of Ferns.

Integrating unrelated things into a coherent whole was one of the arts of the Celtic bard, and Soul Friends pointed their followers toward a similar unified vision. The great stone crosses scattered across the Celtic world became focal points for this unity in multiplicity, a viewpoint the Celtic Christians developed through their understanding of the nature of the Triune God and the created world.

What Can You Learn from the Envisioners?

The Druids, bards, and shamans shaped the ancient Celts in three ways: by guarding and passing on a legacy of folk memory; by introducing the visible world to the invisible one; and by receiving visions of the future and calling forth its potential in the present moment. We too need to be shaped in these ways—and we need to pass this vision along to others.

In our day, this perspective may seem "New Age," but as Christians, we need not fear what is actually the wisdom of the past. The Hebrew Bible (the Old Testament) speaks of "seers," a tiny minority of the population who could see clearly what was going to happen to a person or a people; they could see into others' spiritual condition and discern, through the law of cause and effect, where that spiritual condition would lead. Later in the Hebrew Scriptures, we read of the prophets. Some of these were false; they may have had psychic powers and sharp intuition, but these gifts were not dedicated to God and the purposes of good. As a result, their psychic world became confused and manipulative. The Scriptures suggest that in order to discern whether a prophet is true or false, we judge the "fruits." In other words, does this envisioner lead others closer to God? Does she help create a world where love rules, where people find it easier to live in harmony? Does she reveal the truth? Or does her work seek to bring her power for herself? Does she deceive others? Does her vision contribute to a world where people argue and disagree, where the weak suffer and the powerful gain still more power?

In the Hebrew Scriptures,
people looked forward
to the promised time,
when spiritual discernment
would be possible for all people:

"I will put my instructions
deep within them,
and I will write them
on their hearts, . . .

> And they will not need
> to teach their neighbors,
> nor will they need
> to teach their relatives,
> saying, 'You should
> know the Lord.' For everyone,
> from the least to the greatest,
> will know me already,"
> says the Lord.
>
> —JEREMIAH 31:33, 34 TLB

When we are rooted in Christ, we need not fear learning from the past. The pagan envisioners remind us that we still need those who connect us to the continuity of memory, people who will help us see a deeper reality, and who will also help us build future potential in the here-and-now. As Soul Friends and Seekers, there are at least eight specific things we can learn from our pagan heritage.

1. Seek the whole story.

You are unlikely to be whole if you do not know your own story as a member of a family or of a people. The bards and shapers who passed on folk memory helped their students know their lives were not meaningless incidents; instead, they were related to those who were before them and around them. The Soul Friend should pass on living memory, the stories and wisdom that have shaped us, including our Christian heritage, our ethnic heritage, our national heritage, and our family heritage. In a variety of ways, all of us come from a long line of inspired folk, and we are stronger when we claim this heritage. The Soul Friend, even if his own heritage is far different from the Seeker's, should aim to see the whole picture and to pass this on to the Seeker.

As an example of this, perhaps the Soul Friend senses that something in the Seeker is not quite as it should be. The Seeker seems to be banging her head against walls, never moving ahead in her spiritual development. The Soul Friend realizes that the Seeker's life is like a single puzzle piece. The Soul Friend glimpses something of the whole picture where the puzzle piece belongs, but the Seeker is not even aware there is a bigger picture. This causes her a sense of futility, if not panic. So the Soul Friend begins to fill in some of the missing pieces. The Soul Friend may introduce the Seeker to other contexts, ways of thinking, and types of temperament. This process will include the past, as well as the present. The Seeker begins to realize she has been trying to fit everything into her own narrow picture. Now, the Seeker can move into a wider world. She begins to breathe more freely as she looks around and sees how her own piece of life can harmonize with other pieces; she goes with the flow. She begins to become whole.

2. Unite this world with the spiritual realm.

The Roman writer Mela wrote that the Druids claimed to know the will of the gods. Lucan, in a rhetorical address to the Druids, declaims, "You assure us that with a new body the spirit reigns in another world—if we understand your hymns, death is halfway through a long life." Stories of the Otherworld gripped the imagination of the people and gave them something to which to aspire.

The Celtic Christians did not let the Otherworld become a no-go area, abandoning it to the devil. Instead, they viewed Jesus as a Door into the Otherworld, the Heaven where angels and saints lived. Sometimes they had amazing visions of this other realm, which generated excitement. They taught Scriptures and prayers about the Otherworld, and in their liturgies, they reenacted heavenly realities. Soul Friends freely focused on saints, angels, the triumphant dying of friends, and resurrection—the entry into Heaven to which a Seeker could aspire.

Earth's crammed with heaven,
And every common bush
afire with God.

—ELIZABETH BARRETT BROWNING

Our lives are so easily dominated by immediate pressures that we often fail to live in the perspective of eternity. Yet we are destined for eternal life, and the purpose of our short stay on Earth is to learn to see Heaven here in this life—and to reflect it to those around us. Focusing only on short-term benefits impoverishes us, even if we do not realize it; a person who has not prepared for death has hardly begun to live.

One of the most important functions of a Soul Friend is to help the Seeker reflect upon everyday experience in the light of Heaven. A contemporary Soul Friend might encourage a Seeker to journey to the borderlands between Earth and Heaven. This can be done through meditations on death, resurrection, or angels; celebrating saints' days; or becoming more aware of "Heaven in the ordinary." As the Seeker becomes acquainted with the wonder of the invisible world, hidden anxieties melt away. He no longer fears losing control. Daily thought and action begin to flow out of a life in God, while the grace of Heaven and the poise of eternity gradually replace emptiness and imbalance.

3. Call forth the potential in people.

You can learn from the ancient Celts how to envision others. Nothing exists that God has not created; just as sexuality can be used for good or evil, so can our minds' abilities.

Celtic Christians armed themselves and their protégés against shamanic spells, and Patrick rebuked shape-shifters

—yet Patrick himself disappeared from the officers the High King sent to ambush him, so that all they saw was a herd of deer. This gave rise to the belief that the Lord had confused their sight, and it is why "St. Patrick's Breastplate" is also known as "The Deer's Cry." This experience echoes that of the Hebrew prophet Elisha, who asked the Lord to blind the eyes of enemy troops come to capture him (and God answered that prayer, too; 2 Kings 6:18).

> Soul has a fluency and energy
> which is not to be caged
> within any fixed form.
>
> —JOHN O'DONOHUE[5]

Although Celtic Christian leaders confronted false shamanism, they refused to allow a forbidden realm to develop. They set Christ's claim on the spirit world, and they took the offensive in the realm of Spirit-filled prophecy. False shamans used created forces to make a person be or do something alien to her God-given self; Christian envisioners, however, crossed the parameters of fear, small-mindedness, group prejudice, low self-esteem, and poor conditioning to give the person God-sight so she could become more truly real. These envisioners had been granted a glimpse of the person's true essence, and now by faith, they called forth her potential into the visible world. Imagine the ability to see an oak tree when looking at an acorn! This is the powerful and creative vision Soul Friends are called to share. (Examples of such prophetic prayer are given in chapter 10.)

4. Value Soul Friends' role in the community

Some people are called to be Soul Friend to a gathered community, a neighborhood, or even an entire people.

Our society is often fragmented. Extended families seldom live close to one another, as they once did, and many communities are transitory, no longer deeply rooted in a shared past. Relationships may seem difficult to sustain. And yet in the midst of this, Soul Friendship can still thrive, perhaps because it is needed all the more. When a Soul Friend is called to minister to an entire community—whether that be a congregation, an academic setting, a nation, or some other form of community, large or small—that relationship can have a powerful transforming effect, working to knit together the broken pieces in our society. The ancient pagan Celts can teach us to recognize and affirm this relationship, to give it space in our modern lives.

5. Sustain and honor memory.

The Druids teach us this important lesson: tradition knows more than it can make explicit in words. This is why young people cannot learn tradition through books or in classrooms; they learn it by living it. Their apprenticeship is their connection to the elders in the family and community.

When the living tradition of a land or a faith is broken, so that the community's children no longer experience it firsthand, tradition can die in a single generation. Many of our countries are in grave danger of such a break today. Younger generations are losing contact with the past. They do not know the stories of their people or their spiritual formation. They do not know how they have come to be who they are. As a result, they often do not know how to relate to what is around them in a way that leads to wholeness. They have lost the skill of listening to the wisdom of the ages.

Memory is the treasury
and guardian of all things.

—CICERO

I believe that a large-scale acceleration of Soul Friendship may be able to avert such a disaster. Not all Soul Friends will feel they are called to hand on the legacy of the past, but those who have a deep foundation in our faith heritage should not shy away from passing on this storehouse of wisdom, in any capacity that is open to them.

6. Draw from and sift the insights of our society's envisioners.

The ancient Celts, including the Christian Celts, did not hesitate to imbibe wisdom from other envisioners. We can rightly do the same, learning from the insights of wise guides such as Carl Jung. Christopher Bryant, in his books *Jung and the Christian Way* and *The River Within,* draws deeply upon Jungian insights to help Christians discover their true journey. In his *Modern Man in Search of a Soul,* Jung helps us see how the rhythms of our souls are meant to fit in with the larger rhythms of creation. (At the same time, however, Dr. Geoffrey Satinova warns against a new form of "gnosis," the idea that certain psychic forces are infallible guides and may be followed unconditionally. Satinova reminds us that all our psychic forces, even the Self that Jung distinguishes from the ego, need a Redeemer; we should not abandon ourselves unconditionally to any of them, for they are all fallen in some way.[10])

7. Communicate with those who follow the practices of modern paganism.

In our world today, politicians and other leaders are sometimes said to consult astrologers and mediums. According to recent research, Britain now has more astrologers and mediums than Christian clergy. As more people in Europe and the United States become disillusioned with Christianity, more and more people are also turning anew to ancient pagan beliefs. This way of thinking is sometimes referred to as "New Age."

We need not fear this movement. Instead, we need Christian guides who are credible to people in the New Age movement, who have the humility to accept there is much we do not know, the patience to focus on the long walk on Wisdom's way, the sensitivity to know what and when to confront, the vision to adapt Christian language and practices to the needs of a new generation, and the winsomeness that marked the Irish saints.

8. Learn the value of storytelling.

Storytelling played an important role in the shaping of the Celtic people. One version of "The Voyage of Bran," for example, states that a local ruler named Mongan (who died c. 625) was told a story by his poet (*fili*) every winter night from Samhain to Beltane.

*Stories make us more alive,
more human,
more courageous,
more loving.*

—MADELEINE L'ENGLE[6]

Celtic storytellers memorized the outlines of the tale and filled in details in an impromptu way. That is no doubt why, when these tales came to be transcribed from the seventh century onward, there were various versions of most of them. Most surviving manuscripts date from the twelfth century, by which time they had accumulated many errors and had a secondhand feel about them. These include *The Book of Leinster* (c. 1160), *The Yellow Book of Lecan* (fourteenth century), and Egerton's *The Dream of Oengus* (an eighteenth-century version of a fifteenth-century manuscript). The earliest of the surviving manuscripts is *The Book of the Dun Cow* (*Lebor na Luidre*), so called after a famous cow that belonged to that great Soul Friend and saint Ciaran of Clonmacnoise. The half of the manuscript that survives contains thirty-seven stories. The chief scribe was a monk at Clonmacnoise monastery named Mael Muire, who was killed by raiders in 1106. Clearly, storytelling continued to play an important role in Celtic society far into the Christian centuries.

This ancient Celtic art has never quite died in Scotland and Ireland, and stories are still part of the *ceilidhs* (traditional Gaelic social gatherings). Recently, the Bible Society of England and Wales has introduced storytelling as part of its work; English Heritage uses storytellers to bring historic sites to life.

Stories are powerful mediums for communicating truth. Stories tend to stick in our heads far longer than other knowledge. They help us organize ideas into meaningful narratives. They allow us to make sense of the world and our lives. They carry within them hidden truths that may open up for us much later in our lives. Jesus knew the power of storytelling; the parables he told, which are recorded in the Gospels, continue to transform our world. And Soul Friends who use storytelling as one of the tools of their trade find it to be an effective one for aiding the spiritual journey.

Summary

Celtic Christians rejected the use of occult forces to manipulate others—but they also recognized a continuing need for envisioners to help people picture God's hand in their past, present, and future. Soul Friends today can use imagination to release a Seeker's fullest potential.

EXERCISES

These exercises are intended for anyone, whether or not you are in a Soul Friendship.

1. When you next travel by car, bus, or foot, bless everything your eye sees—the energy of motors, humans, trees. Bless as well the sorrow for what spoils them (for example, mindless rush or pollution). Practice trying to see as God sees, not projecting the distorting demands of your ego on places or people.

2. Create a flowchart, drawing or naming the significant stages in the life of your family, your community, or your nation. What gaps in the story do you see? Plan ways to fill in the gaps.

3. Write your own obituary, looking at your life from the perspective of eternity. What was most significant in it from that point of view?

4. Read stories about the Celtic saints—Patrick, Brigid, Columba, for instance. Then choose an episode from the life of your favorite Celtic saint that has lessons for a Seeker or someone else you know. Try writing the story in your own words or record-

ing it. Revise it to give it more flow and human interest. Revise it again so that the material builds up to and does not detract from the main point. What is that main point?

Read More

Anam Cara: A Book of Celtic Wisdom by John O'Donohue (HarperCollins, 2009) connects the reader with the treasures of wisdom, both Christian and pre-Christian, that lie within the Celtic soul. It is beautifully written by an Irish poet and scholar.

Notes

1. Peter Berresford Ellis. *The Ancient World of the Celts* (New York, NY: Barnes and Noble, 1999), p. 121.

2. John and Caitlin Matthews. *The Little Book of Celtic Wisdom* (London, UK: Pavilion, 2003).

3. Eleanor Hull. *The Poem-Book of the Gael: Translations from Irish Gaelic Poetry* (London, UK: Chatto & Windus, 1912), p. 54.

4. Patrick Connella, trans. *The Poems of Amergin* (Dublin, Ireland: Ossianic Society, 1857).

5. John O'Donohue. *Anam Cara: A Book of Celtic Wisdom* (New York, NY: HarperCollins, 2009).

6. Madeleine L'Engle. *The Rock That Is Higher: Story as Truth* (New York, NY: Crown, 2018).

4

Discernment

Insights from Saint Morgan

(the fourth and fifth centuries after Christ)

For the early followers of Christ, confession was a practical and intimate practice that kept their community healthy. Confession was a two-way street, with both sides involved in finding a way to discern the reality of the situation more clearly. As time went by, however, the sacrament of confession came to mean that priests merely pronounced absolution of sins and prescribed penances or rules according to set formulas. Mutual discernment no longer had a role to play.

Today we are turning back to a more ancient practice, one that requires an active and reciprocal relationship between two people. This form of confession takes into account that the repentance of sins involves not only confession but a specific turning around in our lives. A Soul Friend's role is to help the Seeker discern for herself both the areas where she needs to repent . . . and what action she should take next.

Nowadays a Soul Friend is sometimes called a co-discerner. Discernment is fundamental both to Soul Friendship and to each person's spiritual journey. The Oxford dictionary traces the root of this word to the old French word *discernier*, which means "to separate out as distinct, to distinguish between alternatives." The root word was connected to the concept of sifting out chaff from grain. Spiritual discernment, in other words, allows us to clearly separate that which is authentic in our lives from that which is false.

Those who are spiritually mature
are able, through practice,
to distinguish

between good and evil.

—HEBREWS 5:14 (AUTHOR'S PARAPHRASE)

Discernment is also the art of identifying God's will in the tangle of decisions that face us as we navigate life's maze. It is the process by which we examine, in the light of our faith and our experience of God's love, that which draws us closer to God and that which pulls us away. As we interact with Scripture, our communities, circumstances, creation, and inner conviction, we gradually discover the indicators of Divine will.

Jesus brought the art of discernment to its perfection; he was able to clearly recognize the Divine Way in his life, and then he consistently followed it: "The Son only does what he sees his Father doing" (John 5:19). This was not an instant or easy process for Jesus, however. Even the Son of God needed to sort out which of his compelling thoughts were from God and which were from an evil source. The story of his temptations in the desert (Luke 4:1–13) reveals that he knew the pull of ambition and the temptation to speed things up in order to avoid heartache. The Gospel also tells us that before he chose his twelve apostles, he needed to spend a night alone on a mountain (Luke 6:12). These times of intense solitude were when Christ practiced careful discernment before moving forward with his life.

> Jesus sought discernment in these areas:
>
> - what shape his mission should take,
> - what his priorities should be,
> - what persons he should choose for his task force,
> - which requests he should say yes or no to,
> - who wanted him for himself, rather than for what they could get out of him.

How Can We Learn to Discern the Father's Will as Jesus Did?

Morgan was an honored Celtic Soul Friend, whose letters of spiritual direction still offer us pertinent guidance. Born somewhere in Britain not long after 350, this lay monk had an educated mind, a wrestler's frame, and a holy heart. In the early 380s, he went to Rome, where folks knew him by the Latin name, Pelagius. There he acquired a reputation as an eloquent teacher.

Morgan was horrified to discover the extent of moral laxity and confusion among the Christians in Rome. He believed Augustine's new teachings about everyone's incurable sinfulness only added to this confusion. The idea that we are all predestined to sin, as Augustine taught, produced an "anything goes" mentality, since people said there was nothing they could do about sin. Morgan opposed such views vehemently. He taught that God gives each person the ability to choose between good and evil, and that each of us has a responsibility to discern and follow our genuine callings in life.[1]

Morgan gathered around himself an influential group from Rome's Christianized aristocracy, educated people who were drawn to study the Bible and pursue holy lives. He became their teacher and guide. Several of his writings and letters as a Soul Friend have been preserved.[2] Eventually, after Alaric conquered Rome in 410, Morgan made his way to Palestine and Africa, where he continued to write his letters of spiritual guidance. He died there not long after 418.

Morgan understood the value of a Soul Friend when it comes to discerning good from evil. He wrote:

> People cannot grow in virtue on their own. We each need companions to guide and direct us on the way of righteousness; without such companions, we are liable to stray from the firm path, and then sink

into the mud of despair. At first, a companion who has achieved a high level of virtue can seem utterly different from oneself. But as friendship grows, one begins to see in the companion a mirror of oneself. The reason is that, in moral capacities, God has created us all the same: we are each capable of achieving the same degree of moral goodness. Once people perceive this truth, they are filled with hope, knowing that in the fullness of time they can share the moral virtue of Christ himself.[3]

Today, Morgan's writings still offer us practical guidance for discovering the foundations of spiritual discernment.

Learn God's general will from Christ's life and teaching.

Matthew's Gospel, chapters 5 through 7, offers a summary of the teachings Jesus gave of four absolute standards of honesty, purity, unselfishness, and love. These provide us with touchstones against which to test our every thought and action. Many thoughts or actions can be eliminated as not being God's will because they are not absolutely honest, pure, unselfish, or loving.

Later in the Christian Scriptures, Saint Paul provided a useful tool for discernment in his list of the fruits of God's Spirit versus the fruits of that which is not of the Spirit

(Galatians 5:19–23). If something is of God, Paul wrote, it will produce fruits such as love, joy, peace, patience, kindness, goodness, faithfulness, humility, and self-control. Something is not of God if it spawns immorality, worship of created or occult things, jealousy, temper, division, and drunken or disorderly behavior. We can discern the value and authenticity of people and things in our lives by the fruits they bear.

Absolute honesty is necessary for perceiving God's will (see, for example, John 1:5; 1 John 3:24; 4:13). If we find ourselves hoping that something we are doing will not be discovered by others—in other words, that it will not come out into the light—it is probably not of God.

> We must be honest
> with ourselves,
> recognizing clearly
> those areas of our lives
> that we have not yielded
> to Christ.
>
> —MORGAN[4]

These requirements are not optional. Nor is it acceptable to embrace some sacrifice that *is* optional—such as celibacy, for example—and to tell ourselves that we then have the right to follow selfish desires in other areas of our lives. We cannot barter goodness!

Use reason to weigh good and bad consequences against each other.

Morgan recommended that a person weigh the good and bad consequences he anticipates are likely to result from each course of action. To do this, it helps to draw up two lists: on the first list, write down what will be the likely consequences if you follow plan A, and on the second list, note the likely consequences if you do *not* follow plan A. Then another two lists may be drawn up for plan B, and so on.

At each moment of choice,
. . . God has given us
two vital tools.
The first is reason:
we can use reason to work out
how God's spiritual law applies
in each and every situation.
The second is prayer:

> we can talk to God,
> asking him to guide our thoughts.
> We can be sure that,
> if we consider every choice
> carefully, and if we seek
> divine guidance, our decisions
> will please God.
>
> —MORGAN TO DEMETRIAS5

Pray about your provisional intentions.

The desire to do God's will is a precondition of finding it. We cannot expect to be able to see the Divine will for our lives if our hearts are already set on a particular action. Instead, we need to be receptive to whatever God wants. A childlike attitude that brings everything out in the open before God makes discernment possible. Zen Buddhism refers to this as the "beginner's mind," an attitude of openness and eagerness for new information, rather than having your mind already made up.

Sense whether your actions bring peace or unease.

If you have embarked on a course of action in good faith, but you find yourself feeling uneasy, anxious, and disturbed, this is a sign that you need to go back to square one; you have not heard the Spirit's voice correctly.

For the Anamchara, this principle means that the Soul Friend does not foster dependency but instead teaches the Seeker to listen to her own heart. In other words, the Soul Friend liberates discernment in the Seeker. In Morgan's writings, he often said, in effect: "Don't ask me. Listen to what is deepest in your heart. Then write it out. If it does not accord with Christ, listen again." Morgan was convinced that Christ frees us to become truly ourselves.

Listen to your conscience, . . .
It works by inducing guilt
when you do wrong,
and by inducing feelings of peace
when you do right.
Confess your sins by describing precisely,
within your own mind,
those actions which induced guilt
during the previous day.
Equally note carefully those actions
which induced peace and tranquility.

—MORGAN TO CELANTIA[6]

Four Things That Hinder Discernment

Discernment is a long, hard process. We can so easily get it wrong. Morgan warned of four things that distort discernment.

Sin binds.

Aware of your own faults and weaknesses, you may assume you won't be able to keep to the path of God's will; you dread failure, so you stop the journey; if you don't move, you can't make a mistake! Morgan called this depression. He seemed to recognize, as does modern medicine, that individuals may not be responsible for their depression, but at the same time, he asserted that people are responsible for the way they respond to depression.

Depression is often linked to what we feed into our unconscious minds. When we feed our bodies, minds, or emotions something that is a substitute for God, we may become addicted; we come to rely on something other than true physical, intellectual, or spiritual nourishment; and as a result, we become unbalanced and depressed. In order to feel better about this, we often tell ourselves that this addictive living is normal, and that a God-centered way of life is abnormal. We associate with others who have addictive lifestyles, and this forms a narcissistic web around our lives.

When we are bound in this way, how can we discern what is reality? Jesus had to use shock language to shake people out of this attitude: "If your eye offends you, pull it out. It is better to go into the kingdom of God with one eye than not at all" (Matthew 18:9).

We may not be responsible for creating the web of lies that surrounds us, but yet we allow ourselves to be comfortable in the midst of it. In order to become free, we have to be willing to take radical action and slice through the sticky strands that keep us bound. We would do well to follow Morgan's advice: be open before God about our lives; bring everything out into the light; stop clinging to that which holds us back.

At each moment of decision,
you must sincerely seek
to discern the will of God.

—MORGAN[7]

Sin multiplies.

Morgan regarded speed as the great enemy of discernment. The more we hurry, the more sin spreads throughout life.

Today, in a society that is pressurized and driven, this enemy is stronger than ever.

We may rush through life because we fear to face what lies under the surface. Or we may rush to acquire money and things or to prove our own worth. In the process, we may take shortcuts with the truth. We start out telling a little white lie, but in order to buttress that falsehood, we have to tell another one, and then another. Our impatience and negligence hurt others. This causes criticism and leads to more damage, which breeds still more misunderstanding. Eventually, we spend more and more of our psychic energy coping with the multiplying grievances. We ask ourselves, why did our lives become so complicated?

Jesus knew it was vital to break this vicious spiral. That is why he told the crowds, "Blessed are the pure in heart. They shall see God." Those who are pure have integrity; their lives have a stillness and calm at their center that prevents them from being pulled in a million hurried directions all at once. And this is why Morgan urged his friends to take time to mull and slowly pray over decisions.

In the teachings
and example of Jesus Christ

> we learn the general principles
> of behavior that pleases God.
>
> —MORGAN[8]

Sin blinds.

Morgan called this complacency. When this sets in, we no longer see people as they really are. We look out at the world as if our own egos were its center, and this skewed perspective distorts everything we view. As far as we are concerned, the world can go to hell in a handbasket, so long as we get what we want.

The Chinese map of the world once showed their own land as the single civilized country in the center of the world, while all the other nations were lumped together as barbarians along the distant edges. All of us tend to have a similar map of reality. I'm reminded of an old Devon man's words to his wife: "All the world's odd except thee and me, and even thee's a bit odd."

Once again, Jesus used strong language to shock people out of this distorted way of seeing: "Before you can remove the speck that is in your brother's eye you need to remove the log that is in your own" (Matthew 7:4).

Sin divides.

Whenever we indulge our selfish cravings—Morgan called this the instant gratification of desires—we avoid taking responsibility for something we were meant to do or say. To protect ourselves from acknowledging this (even to ourselves) we erect defenses within ourselves; eventually, these walls not only hide us from the truth, but they also become barriers between ourselves and others. When we live behind barricades, how can we discern what is beyond them? How can we perceive what is true and what is false?

Jesus was quite clear that judging others is a sinful perspective. "Forgive your enemies," he said (Matthew 5:44).

No two true duties conflict. What is best for others will ultimately be best for us as well.

But when we try to serve two masters, we fail to do right by either. We cannot pretend to follow Jesus if we are putting ourselves first.

> If you are half-hearted . . .
> the devil will take a firm grip
> of one half of the heart, and use it
> to subjugate the other . . .
> If you constantly try to compromise,

> finding some middle path between
> the way of Christ and the way of the world,
> you will become confused and lost.
> Jesus never compromised:
> neither should you.

—MORGAN TO A NEW CHRISTIAN[9]

Life is never simple, though. Morgan pointed out that even if we avoid the snares of the evil one within our minds, a decision made in good faith may still have bad consequences. Life's net of interconnections is complex, and what is good for someone else may seem harmful to our own interests. We are not immune from things going wrong, even when we have made decisions with a pure conscience. We are responsible to make decisions with a pure conscience—but we are not responsible for the outcomes.

Saint Ignatius's Insights into Discernment

Over the centuries, others have built on Morgan's ground rules for discernment. Ignatius Loyola, a Basque who lived in the fifteenth century, became almost a cult name for discernment and spiritual direction.

"His insights have a Celtic feel about them," said someone during a group discussion.

"Of course," piped up a former Catholic nun, "that's because he was a Celt."[10]

Ignatius was a sharp contrast to the typical Latin, continental spiritual leader of his day. Whereas continental thinkers would typically live to think, Ignatius—like the pragmatic Anglo-Saxons—thought to live. His approach was very practical.

My friend the former nun, however, was not as interested in ethnic origins as in style. "He was a Celt in two ways," she insisted. "He was passionately red-blooded, and he went into the marketplace." In other words, his perception of life was physical, and he was not afraid to mingle in the real world.

That is most certainly true. Inigo, as his family called him, was passionate with women, in jousting, in socializing, and in warfare—until he was invalided out of the military with a nearly fatal leg injury. After bearing agonizing operations with heroic courage, through his bedside books he began a dalliance with the saints. He discovered that flirting with women and flirting with saints affected his spirit in clearly different ways.

Ignatius transposed his passion from carousing, warfare, and women—what some people call the high life—to Christ and the still higher life of the Spirit. Soon, he founded a team of Christ-followers, and he worked out spiritual exercises that helped his old flames and friends "in the marketplace" as much as they did churchy people. These exercises were a roadmap for gaining discernment. In the centuries since then, his *Spiritual Exercises* has proved to be a classic in spiritual direction, and many have followed his roadmap.

Our only desire and our one choice
should be this: I want
and I choose what better leads
to God's deepening life in me.

—IGNATIUS OF LOYOLA[11]

Ignatius's starting point was the same as Morgan's: each person has the ability to choose between good and evil. But you don't question certain basic choices, he said, since they have already been made. If you are married, for example, in most cases you needn't agonize over whether God wants you to be married. Instead, provided your marriage is healthy and loving, you stick with your spouse through thick and thin, because God has already made clear in Scripture that this is the Divine will. That still leaves you with many other choices. The next step is to be completely open to whatever God desires for you. The third step is to say no to any choice that is evil (that is, which goes against the moral teachings of the Bible, summarized in the commandments to love the Lord with all your mind, soul, and body, and to treat others as you would want to be treated). The fourth step is to wait on God (ideally in a retreat) until God speaks with a voice so clear you cannot mistake it, as when Christ called the apostles to follow him. God's revelation has its own timing, and if we are sensitive to the Spirit, we can sense when this is. When no such special time of revelation comes to us, however, Ignatius taught that we should not be afraid to use prayerful imagination.

Again echoing Morgan, Ignatius suggested that we should also use our reason—our intellectual abilities—to work out a right course of action. To do this, we should become tranquil, clarify the decision to be made, and then look at it from this point of view: Why were we created? What is our purpose on Earth? How does this choice connect with that purpose? From this perspective, we can weigh the advantages and disadvantages of each option.

These steps in discernment are practical and helpful, but, like Morgan, Ignatius recognized that they are not foolproof. Evil and deceptive spirits can lead us astray. Delusions and confusions can afflict us. Whether we believe these come from the devil, as Ignatius did, or from psychic and spiritual forces within our own minds, how do we circumnavigate these dangers?

Ignatius dealt with this problem in his "Rules for the Discernment of Spirits," which he appended to his *Spiritual Exercises*. After much testing within his own experience (you might say Ignatius followed the scientific method based on observable results, with his own life as the foundation for his data), he came up with two indicators of the good or the bad way, which again echo Morgan. Instead of using Morgan's terms of "guilt" and "peace," Ignatius used the terms "desolation" and "consolation." If our intended choices produce desolation, he said, we should reconsider our choice. If they produce consolation, we should proceed.

Fears about our own resources, depression, self-pity, and a sense of diminished strength and well-being are all forms of desolation that can lead us to reconsider our path. However, these feelings can also keep us stuck in zones of false comfort. According to Ignatius, the devils use our fears to afflict us with anxiety, confusion, and distractions, and to probe and test us until they find our limits.

Ignatius's advice was practical and down to earth: Never make a change during a time of desolation. Instead, remain firm in the course you were on before the desolation beset you. He advised people to sometimes combat desolation with penance, but other times to fight off desolation with rest, fun, or some form of nourishment (whether physical, emotional, intellectual, or spiritual). Although desolation is from the devil, taught Ignatius, and can be brought on by our own spiritual slackness, God can also use it to help us find a deeper understanding of ourselves, or to test and build our characters. God can reveal the truth through all things, so long as our response is to open ourselves like flowers before God.

Meanwhile, consolation, which always comes directly from God, gives us a deep sense of being at peace in the will of God. It brings us courage, strength, healing tears, and inspiration. Anything that shakes our commitment to God is not the right direction to go, but anything that strengthens our commitment is from God. The danger in consolation, however, is that when we experience it, we may coast along in our own strength or become conceited. So Ignatius advised people to humble themselves whenever they felt especially blessed with consolation.

Ignatius concluded that a person who fundamentally wants God's way will feel desolation when she sins or when the devil tempts her, and consolation when God's will is being done in her life. The reverse, however, is true of a person who at heart does not want God's way. That person may feel apparent consolation or pleasure in wrongdoing, but desolation and distress when influenced by God's Spirit.

Ignatius described one other complication on the road to discernment. Although true consolation comes from God,

Ignatius taught, the devil can mimic it in order to lead us away from our true path. So how can we discern the difference between a true, God-given consolation and a false one?

According to Ignatius, pseudo consolations never end up with us being closer to God, but true consolations do. Pseudo consolation can never give the deep interior peace and genuine exterior unity with others that is the fruit of God's Spirit. The devil can never fake unconditional love.

A few Soul Friends have a particular gift of discerning spirits. Soul Friends need to become familiar with these ways of improving discernment in their own lives, if they are to use them to facilitate discernment in a Seeker. No two situations in life, nor the makeup of any two individuals, are identical. So, as a co-discerner—someone who supports and directs the Seeker as he determines the Divine will for his life—the Soul Friend will be very attentive to the course of action that seems to uniquely fit each individual.

Summary

The basic work of a Soul Friend is to help a Seeker to discern God's will. Morgan advised that we can learn to do this by eliminating choices that do not line up with Christ's teachings, by figuring out the likely good and bad consequences of any intended action, and by observing which of these brings us peace or disquiet. Areas that are still resistant need to be prayerfully examined in the light of the power of evil, in its various modes, to blind and ensnare us. *The Spiritual Exercises* by Ignatius of Loyola can further help us understand Morgan's ideas about discernment.

EXERCISES
For both Soul Friends and Seekers

1. Think of a choice you have to make. What would your choice be if you had to make it immediately, off the top of your head? Now draw up two lists of likely consequences if you do and if you do not follow plan A. Repeat this for plan B. Do the results support your initial choice?

2. Think about your fundamental choice, the thing that lies at the deepest level beneath your options. This may not be immediately clear to you, but as you take time to ponder, it will reveal itself. What are you truly being asked to choose between? Are you clear you want God's will more than anything else?

3. Recall an experience when it was hard to know what you really felt. Can you put a name to your different feelings now? What can you learn from this in the light of the guidelines given by both Morgan and Ignatius?

4. Recall an experience of spiritual defeat. What dragged you down? What tactics did "the devil" (the

forces of destruction) employ to distract you from the truth?

5. Recall an experience of victory that brought consolation. What choices or inspirations brought you closer to God?

6. Think of a choice you have to make in your current life. How would you counsel another person who came to you for advice about the same choice?

7. Think of another choice you have to make. If you were on your deathbed, looking back at this moment of your life, which choice would you wish you had made?

Read More

Pelagius: Life and Letters by B. R. Rees (Boydell Press, 2004). This book will allow you to discover more about Morgan's teaching by reading his words for yourself.

Always Discerning: An Ignatian Spirituality for the New Millennium by Joseph A. Tetlow, S.J. (Loyola, 2016). This book teaches how we can implement discernment into not only life's big decisions but also into the more mundane choices we encounter every day.

Notes

1. Augustine and other figures in the Western church attacked Pelagius for his criticisms of their writings. He was accused of heresy and twice cleared of this charge at church synods. The Pope also declared him innocent of these charges but then retracted this decision under pressure from leading theologians such as Augustine. A synod in Africa then declared Pelagius to be heretical. Unfortunately, synods at this time were influenced by worldly politics of the very sort that Pelagius wanted to eradicate. However, no council representing the universal church condemned him, and Pelagius reaffirmed his allegiance to all the teachings of the Holy Catholic Church at one of these synods. As the universal church continues to weigh these things today, there is a growing conviction that Augustine himself may have been

heretical in teaching that the material and human creation (including sex) were inherently evil, and that Pelagius may have been misrepresented. For a full treatment of this issue see *Pelagius: A Reluctant Heretic* by B. R. Rees (Woodbridge, UK: Boydell Press, 1991).

2. See *The Letters of Pelagius and His Followers*, edited by B.R. Rees (Woodbridge, UK: Boydell Press, 1991). Robert Van der Weyer's *The Letters of Pelagius, Celtic Soul Friend* (Alresford, UK: Arthur James, 1995) is another popular edited paraphrase of Morgan's letters.

3. B. R. Rees. *The Letters of Pelagius and His Followers* (Woodbridge, UK: Boydell Press, 1991).

4. Ibid.

5. Ibid.

6. Ibid.

7. Ibid.

8. Ibid.

9. Ibid.

10. Before the time of Christ, the Celts mingled with the people of the Iberian Peninsula, who might be called the aborigines of Europe. This people then spread outward; some people think that the Basque people have inherited their language. That seems doubtful, since research into the Basque and Celtic languages fails to uncover obvious connections. What

seems more likely is that that the Basques are a parallel people and that both they and the Celts have retained certain primal qualities in common. Certainly, the Basques are a remnant of prehistoric populations, and are as distinct from the continental peoples as are the Celts. See Henri Hubert's *The History of the Celtic People* (London, UK: Bracken Books, 1993), p. 77.

11. David L. Fleming, S.J. *Draw Me into Your Counsel: A Literal Translation and a Contemporary Reading of the Spiritual Exercises* (Brighton, MA: Institute of Jesuit Sources, 1996), p. 27.

5

Fostering

Irish Insights into Soul Friendship

(the fifth to eighth centuries after Christ)

here are two threads in the ancient Irish Soul Friendship tradition: fosterers created by families for children and young adults, and monasteries' provision of Soul Friends to spiritual seekers. Both of these forms of Soul Friendship kindled warm bonds of human affection. Although the roles of foster parent and Soul Friend are separate in our modern society, the ancient Irish experience can inspire all Soul Friends to grow in a love that fosters within a Seeker all that is of God.

Soul Friends for Young People

Sixth-century Irish families with some degree of wealth usually employed foster parents to help bring up their children. The foster parents were not a married couple that substituted for the physical parents if the need arose—as we usually think of foster parents today—but a cherished supplement to the parents' care, individuals who were often widowed or unmarried celibates. Foster parents did not live with the families, as British nannies did; instead, the children would live with the foster parents for quite long periods. As the children shared in the foster parents' lives, they would learn to cook, fish, pray, repeat stories, make relationships, and grow confident in both practical living and in the inner life.

In the early days of the Irish church, foster parents were the ones who guided a young person into adulthood. As Christianity spread, parents sometimes sensed their child was being called to a spiritual vocation, and they would place this child under the care of a holy hermit or nun who lived in the district. A good foster parent would be both worldly wise and spiritually wise. The medieval *Lives of Irish*

Saints implies that many Christ-followers continued to visit their foster parents as long as they lived.

Do nothing
without counsel.

—THE RULE OF COLUMBANUS[1]

Monastic Soul Friends

The wider family of the tribe was the central spoke of Irish society, the center point that focused the community. With this basic structure at the foundation of their mental paradigm, the Irish readily and easily took to their hearts the concept of the monastic family, with its spiritual father or mother known as an abbot or abbess. In later centuries, those terms—abbess and abbot—became over-formalized, losing the sense of their original meaning. As with *ammas* and *abbas* of the desert, the terms "mama" or "papa" more accurately convey how the Irish people regarded these dear folk.

Since Jesus' "tribe"—he and the apostles he chose—numbered thirteen, the Irish considered this to be the ideal family size for a new monastery. Quite often, though, monasteries soon grew into communities numbering hundreds. When they grew to such a size, the abbot or abbess could not realistically be a Soul Friend to every monk, let alone to visitors, so other individuals were allocated this role. Some of these people were ordained, and others were not.

As large monasteries became widely established, young people who were called to the monastic life might be placed under a Soul Friend in a monastery. In the early days of the monasteries, Christ-followers often experienced a depth of trust and a passion for growth that was like a glowing fire—eager, hot, and all-consuming. A trainee monk was expected to pour out his soul each day to the senior who was his Soul Friend. This allowed things that clogged relationships with God or the brothers to be immediately identified, and then confessed and forgiven.

Monks with a vocation for spiritual guidance also became Soul Friends to people outside the monasteries. The spiritual life was very real to the ancient Irish, and many people were enthusiastic about following God in their ordinary jobs.[2] Many of the stories about the Irish saints that have been handed down to us sprang out of these relationships between the saints and their Soul Friends. These stories offer us insights into this way of friendship. They reveal that Soul Friendships of various kinds were normal, and also that the Irish enjoyed more relaxed relationships between men and women than existed in the Egyptian deserts. The individuals' stories that follow are presented in chronological order to reflect the developing process.³

Spiritual mentoring
can be seen as a significant
part of what historians
have come to call
the flowering of Ireland.

—EDWARD SELLNER⁴

Patrick (390 to 461): "Every Benefit to Soul and Spirit"

Patrick was a Briton, but we include him here as an adopted Irishman. His own two writings tell us little about his personal friends, but the *Lives of Irish Saints,* written during the Middle Ages, gives us greater detail (albeit filled with what is likely legendary exaggeration).

At the age of thirty, Patrick is thought to have set out for Rome. On his way through Gaul, he stayed at the monastery of Germanus, who was a God-inspired bishop. In all likelihood, Patrick stayed with Germanus for many years and was mentored by him. The *Lives* states that with Germanus, Patrick "learned, loved, and treasured wholeheartedly knowledge, wisdom, purity, and every benefit to soul and spirit."

Ciaran (About 512 to 545): "There Was Complete Union Between Us"

"The Life of Ciaran of Clonmacnois" portrays him as "blazing with light and instruction." Ciaran himself, nevertheless, needed a Soul Friend of his own, and the *Lives* reveals that Ciaran placed himself under the guidance of Finnian, spiritual father of the prominent monastery at Clonard.

While Ciaran was there, a local ruler brought his daughter, who had taken vows, to be discipled at the monastery, and Finnian entrusted her to Ciaran. Together, Ciaran and the young woman memorized psalms—but all the while, Ciaran guarded against sexual temptation by looking only at her feet! On another, later occasion, a family Ciaran had helped gave their whole estate over to him. In return, he agreed to give them spiritual guidance. The family's beautiful daughter was included in this arrangement—but only under the condition that she dedicate her body as well as her soul to Christ. These two stories show that healthy boundaries need to be established in every friendship, especially those that exist between members of the opposite sex. If even a holy man like Ciaran knew he was vulnerable to sexual temptation, how much more all of us should be on guard against any opportunity where our egos might misuse a Seeker's vulnerability!

This same family's estate soon had a group of monks as its hub and became known as a monastery, which was common with many estates in Ireland at that time. When the time came for Ciaran to move on from Finnian's tutelage, he offered this monastery, whose site is unknown, to Finnian. The aging Finnian refused the gift, and instead offered his own monastery to Ciaran. This act of trust and love made Ciaran burst into tears.

Finnian took this as a sign. "From now on there will be complete union between us, and whoever tries to spoil our union shall possess nothing on Earth or in Heaven."

"Yes, let it be as you say," Ciaran agreed.

Ciaran and Finnian separated, and Ciaran went next to Enda, the great teacher of the Irish Church at the Aran monastery, "to commune with him." Ciaran and Finnian, however, remained still united in spirit; in this story, we see how two Soul Friends may cease to meet and yet retain deep spiritual bonds forever in their hearts. Those bonds can be reactivated as needed.

Ciaran made friends throughout Ireland. According to the *Lives*, these friends included Columba of Iona; Enda, his guide on Aran Island; his colleague Senan of Scattery Island; and his close friend Kevin of Glendalough. All these men were deeply spiritual, and we can imagine that their friendship kindled Ciaran's own relationship with God to grow ever deeper and brighter.

> The heartfelt counsel
> of a friend is as sweet
> as perfume and incense.
>
> —PROVERBS 27:9 NLT

Ita (About 570): Foster Mother of the Saints

An eighth-century poem by Alcuin describes Ita, who lived some fifty years after Brigid, as "the foster mother of the saints of Ireland." As we have already discussed, the ancient Irish often placed their children with foster parents who combined the roles of nanny and teacher. When Christianity took root in Ireland, the element of prayer guide was added to this role, and foster parents were chosen for their ability to make saints out of promising children and young adults. Ita was a shining example of this.

Before she could become a spiritual foster mother, however, Ita, like the Mothers of the Desert, had to gain mastery of herself. She learned to fast and pray with great effect even as a child, but her baptism of fire came when she was a teenager.

One day, Ita told her parents she wanted to become a nun. Her father, who was related to the rulers of Tara, vehemently opposed her decision. Ita calmly and confidently told everyone who was upset about this, "Leave my father alone for a while. If nobody pressures him, he will come round in his own time. In fact, he will order me to take vows based on his own conviction, for he will be compelled by my Lord Jesus Christ to let me go wherever I wish to serve God."

Not long after this, Ita fasted for three days and three nights, during which time she saw the devil waging war against her. She resisted, and eventually, the devil left her with these words: "Alas, Ita, you will free yourself from me, and many others too will be delivered."

That same night, Ita's father dreamed that an angel spoke to him: "Why do you forbid your daughter to be a virgin for Christ's sake? She will be a great and famous virgin before God and God's saints, and she will be the protector of many on the Day of Judgment. You will let her be a nun, and you will let her go wherever she wants to in order to serve Christ. She will serve God in another people, and she will be the mother of that people." Ita's father immediately gave his blessing, even if it meant she would become a spiritual mother to a hostile clan.

As we consider this story, keep in mind what virginity meant to a young woman during this era. It was not a denial of her sexuality but instead an opportunity for her to have a life unthreatened by death in childbirth. Virginity truly protected her and allowed her to thrive spiritually and intellectually in ways she never could have as a wife and biological mother.

God directed Ita to live among the neighboring people of Ui Conaill, where she and some companions established a convent. Young women flocked to her from all over Ireland, as did the local people and their ruler, who offered her more land. Blessings flowed from Ita to the people, and they showered the convent with gifts. This did not deflect Ita from living simply, though she had to learn not to punish her body with too much fasting. She always refused to buy food, and the stories tell us that an angel persuaded her to eat the food that was given to her.

The story of her life in *Irish Lives* gives us glimpses of her ability to discern the truth. This prevented much time being wasted in her spiritual direction of others. For example, one of her nuns secretly had sex with a man one night. The next day, Ita summoned her, told her exactly when and where she had transgressed, and urged her to guard her virginity. This prophetic word brought a change of heart; the nun willingly undertook exercises to build up her ability to master sexual temptations, and thereafter she succeeded in living a life that was wholly committed to her vocation. Another of Ita's protégés, a nun who lived at a distance in Ita's native Connacht, also secretly took a lover. From far away, Ita knew even this, and she requested that the nun be released to visit her. When Ita confronted the woman with what she had done, the woman was shocked into repentance. She made restitution for her actions and renewed her commitment to her chosen way of life.

Many people came to Ita to confess their sins, even though they knew she would not let them off lightly. They understood she would administer discipline that would require them to make restitution to a wronged person, which would at the same time strengthen their ability to overcome weaknesses. Ita had an awesome authority, but she also was a loving and loveable woman. She did not hand out penances for their own sake, as punishment. Her goal was always to strengthen and build up both the individual and the community.

A man once confessed to her that he had killed his brother. Because she sensed that he was truly sorry before God for his terrible sin, she told him, "If you carry out my counsel, you will have a happy death." A later incident with this same man shows that Ita did not bury her head in the sand when something went wrong; her policy was always to face evil squarely—and then overcome it with the creative power of goodness. When Ita got news that the man had been killed in battle, she told a friend, "I promised that man he would have a happy end. Go to the place of devastation and call upon him in God's name and in my name to rise up. I believe he will come and meet you." According to the story, the man did just that and then lived a long time longer.

As Soul Friends, we can learn from Ita to fast and pray until we win the battles in our own souls. Only then will we have strength and insights to offer the Seekers who come to us.

Encourage each other
and build each other up.

—1 THESSALONIANS 5:11 NLT

Findbarr (About 560 to 610): "Resurrection Together"

When Findbarr was still a boy, his parents dedicated him to God and sent him to live under the guidance of a Soul Friend named Lochan. One day, a rich man named Fidach arrived and asked Lochan to be his Soul Friend. Instead of responding as Fidach expected, Lochan said to him, "Kneel to that little lad there."

Fidach, insulted at the thought of kneeling to a boy as young as Findbarr, hemmed and hawed. "If I take Findbarr to be my Soul Friend, will you do the same?" he finally asked.

To Fidach's surprise, Lochan said he would. Both men knelt before Findbarr and asked him to be their Soul Friend.

The young Findbarr, with a delicate wisdom beyond his years, then told his tutor, "Will you please be responsible for soul-befriending Fidach and his offspring in return for teaching me the psalms?"

His words reveal a canny humor. Families were expected to pay for their children's fostering, and the arrangement required a careful mixture of goodwill and negotiation. By requesting that Lochan take responsibility for Fidach's Soul Friendship—giving back to Lochan the fees this wealthy man would undoubtedly pay for the relationship—Findbarr had gracefully honored his mentor while at the same time relieving his own family of the responsibility of paying Lochan for Findbarr's tutoring.

The Irish drew inspiration from the desert Soul Friends—but the Irish Anamcharas were often very different from the desert ascetics. Instead, the Irish Soul Friend relationship often had a homely, earthy flavor. Nor did Irish Anamcharas have to be older than their disciples, as this delightful legend reveals.

Irish Christians who took vows often placed themselves under a tutor who trained them in a total life experience of head, heart, and practical knowledge. Another story from Findbarr's life indicates that the fees for this intensive training could be paid either in money or in spiritual kind.

When Findbarr grew older, he moved on from Lochan's home in order to study the Gospel of Matthew and the Acts of the Apostles with Bishop MacCuirb. In due course, the bishop requested a stipend for his instruction.

"How much do you require?" Findbarr asked.

The payment the bishop requested was not what Findbarr expected. "I ask that the resurrection of us both may be in the same place on the Day of Judgment," was the bishop's answer.

"You will have your wish," answered the prophetic Findbarr, "for you will be buried in the same place as I am, and we will have our resurrection together."

As Soul Friends, we should take Bishop MacCuirb's priorities to heart. Although our practical needs are real, spiritual rewards can outweigh them.

Still later in his life, Findbarr went to live near Loch Iree. He started a school there, whose tutor was Eolang, and Findbarr's sister, along with many other male and female students came to study at the school. Eventually, Findbarr himself moved on yet again to build cells by the lake at Gougane Barra, where new people devoted themselves to Christ under his guidance.

While he was there, Bishop MacCuirb died. Now Findbarr himself no longer had a Soul Friend. He decided to make an unannounced return visit to Loch Iree and ask his old friend Eolang to be his Soul Friend. Eolang had a premonition that Findbarr was coming, and he did a wise thing.

When Findbarr arrived, he asked the guest master if he could go straight to his friend. Eolang, however, had already told the guest master to arrange for Findbarr to bathe and rest overnight, and to instruct him in the morning to go with his traveling group to cells some miles away for a few days of quiet reflection.

Eolang then came to Findbarr. Kneeling, he placed himself and his community under Findbarr's oversight.

Findbarr was overwhelmed and tears sprang to his eyes. "This was not what I had intended," he told Eolang. "I meant to place everything, my soul and my community, under your guidance."

"Let go of your intention, for this is the will of God," replied Eolang. "You are dear to God and you are greater than myself. I ask only one thing, that our resurrection will be in the same place."

"That wish will be fulfilled," Findbarr assured him, "but I am still troubled about the Soul Friendship." Findbarr knew that he needed someone to replace Bishop MacCuirb's role in his life, and the arrangement Eolang was proposing indicated that instead, Findbarr would be acting as Eolang's mentor.

"You will receive today a Friend worthy of yourself," Eolang assured him. Then he took Findbarr's hand and offered it to God, placing it in the Divine hand. "Lord, take this man to yourself," he prayed, and, according to the *Lives,* Christ began at that moment "leading him to heaven." The story continues that from that time, no one could look at Findbarr's hand because of its radiance—after all, God had directly grasped it—and so he always wore a glove.

As Soul Friends, we too can learn a lesson from Eolang. Soul Friendship can be a reciprocal relationship; we may learn as much from our Seekers as they do from us. And whenever we feel the need for a human Soul Friend, we can have faith that we will be led directly by God's own hand. We are never meant to depend more on any human being than we do on God. Our spiritual foster parents guide us into maturity— and then it is fitting that they leave us. Death, geographical distance, and other circumstances can come between us and our Soul Friends, but Soul Friends are intended to be only provisional helpers. They point us toward Christ, and they give us glimpses of Divine love. They are companions on the Way, but Jesus Christ himself is the Way, the Truth, and the Life.

As each one has received a
special gift, employ it
in serving one another

> as good stewards of the
> multifaceted grace of God.
>
> —1 PETER 4:10 NASB

Maedoc (Died 626): Soul Friendship Is a Gift

Maedoc was trained at St. David's Welsh school, returned to his native Ireland, and founded communities at Ferns and elsewhere. Several centuries later, these various communities produced biographies of their founder, which are mostly comprised of legends. One thing that shines out through all these accounts is Maedoc's great capacity for friendship. He was thought to have retained a lifelong friendship with his tutor David, with Molaise, with his colleague Columba, and with Ita.

According to tradition, Maedoc's birth was foretold by Ireland's chief sage, Finn Mac Cumaill. Shortly before Finn was buried at Ferns, he is said to have uttered this prophetic poem:

> *Ferns of the green strand!*
> *Excellent will be the man who will own it.*
> *Soul friends will come from here,*
> *It will be a place dear to God.*
> *Maedoc with his company will come*
> *Like the sheen of the sun after showers.*

A company did indeed come there to Maedoc for spiritual direction, and many went on from there to be Soul Friends to others. At the time when Maedoc had returned to Ireland after some years with David's Welsh community, he confided that he wished he had asked David who should be his Soul Friend on his return to Ireland. He continued to be so concerned that a group of brothers prepared a boat to take them back to Wales to consult with David about this. They were about to leave when the crew went on strike, and the elements erupted. Miraculously, Maedoc strode through the pounding waves; God taught him to live without human dependency. A Divine messenger told him: "You need no Soul Friend but the God of the elements, for he understands the thoughts and secrets of every person."

Once Maedoc learned that lesson, God gave him a most beautiful friendship with a holy monk named Molaise. This came as a gift—not as a right to be clutched—and the two men recognized when God was bringing their relationship to an end. Though Maedoc and Molaise loved each other deeply, they knew from the start that as God led each of them onward, it might mean separation. One day, as they sat praying at the foot of two trees, they asked Jesus, "Is it your will that we should part or that we should remain together until we die?" There must have been either a tree-cutting project or a gale, for one of the trees fell to the south and the other to the north. They took this as a clear indication that one of them must go south to found a new community, and the other should go north. They kissed, embraced, and said farewell. Maedoc went south to Ferns, and Molaise went north to Devenish.

We can learn from Maedoc about letting go of friendships. If we are clutching at a special friendship, or if we are jealous in case others replace us in our friend's affections, we may be sure God is calling us to let go of that friendship. The willingness to receive friendship as a gift and to let God show when and if we meet together is vital to true Soul Friendship.

After Maedoc settled at Ferns, many people sought his guidance, as Finn had prophesied. An episode that throws light on this soul-friending process concerns some Christ-followers who wanted to know where their place of resurrection would be. One way in which spiritual direction came to Irish Christians in their journey through life was through the discovery of their place of resurrection. This was the place to which they were called, which would become their spiritual home, their place of burial, and the place where they would continue to pray for others after their death. This principle still seems to apply today, and the first exercise at the end of this chapter explores this. For some people, the geographical location is less important than being in the right context in other ways at death.

When the people prayed about this matter, God told them to visit Maedoc. Since these folk had been drawn to

Maedoc at Ferns, he tried to discern whether that was to be their place of resurrection. So he asked them, "Did any of you hear a bell ring when you arrived?" They did not. Maedoc sensed that since no bell at Ferns had rung, their place of resurrection would be somewhere else, yet still within the region to which they had been drawn. So he walked with them to a rise from which they could see miles of countryside. Speaking out what the Spirit put in his mind, he pointed in a certain direction and told them that would be their place of resurrection.

> You can't possibly embrace
> that new relationship,
> that new companion, . . .
> that new friendship,
> or that new life you want,
> while you're still holding on
> to . . . the last one. Let go . . .
> and allow yourself to embrace
> what is waiting for you.
>
> —STEVE MARABOLI[5]

Samthann (Died 739): Prayer Guide

Samthann, Abbess of Clonbroney, was married before becoming a nun, and her foster father was a king. She was given leadership of a monastery through a prophetic vision given to Funecha, the foundress of Clonbroney monastery. Funecha saw Samthann as a spark of fire that grew to a great flame and blazed over the monastery. She understood this to mean that Samthann was burning with the Holy Spirit, and that through her, the monastery would come alight with the power and wonders of God.

So Samthann was made its abbess, and she is remembered for her wisdom. Men and women, laypeople and monks flocked to her for advice and guidance. She was powerful in prayer and ministry.

A nobleman named Flann spent much time studying with her and asked her advice about ways of praying. He wondered whether a person should pray lying down, sitting, or standing. Samthann replied, "A person may pray in every position." A teacher whose enthusiasm outweighed his wisdom also came to her and proposed to give up study in order to use the time to pray. The wise woman asked him a question: "What, if it is not study, can prevent your mind from wandering all over the place as you pray?" The same man told her that he intended to go abroad on a pilgrimage. "By all means travel overseas," she advised, "if God cannot be found on this side of the sea. But since God is near to all those who call upon him, we have no need to cross the sea."

Samthann was the Soul Friend of Mael-Ruain who, as we shall see in chapter 10, was one of the leaders of an eighth-century reform movement known as Friends of God (Celi De). Samthann and Mael-Ruain's friendship came about in this way: A traveling peddler used to carry Samthann's greetings to the Friends of God in Munster. On one occasion she made him promise not to add or subtract one word from her message: "Tell Mael-Ruain that he is my most favored priest of the desert. Another thing, ask him whether he accepts women for confession, and will he accept my Soul Friendship?" Samthann knew how to encourage a shy young Christ-follower with leadership potential!

As soon as the young monk Mael-Ruain received the message, he stood up and praised God, stretching out his arms in the shape of the cross. When asked if he would accept a woman as a Soul Friend, he blushed deeply, bowed three times to the Trinity, remained in silence, and then said, "Yes!"

When Samthann learned of his reply, she is reported to have said, "I think something will come of that youth."

These Irish Soul Friends seem so human as well as holy, homespun yet wise, both humorous and hospitable. They warm our hearts, they speak to us across the centuries, and they invite us to foster Christ in others. Increasing numbers of today's Christ-followers are following the example of Irish Soul Friends and choosing to live lives of prayer and reflection in quiet places. Many others seek out such people, either in a short-term or a longer-term Soul Friend relationship.

Summary

The early Irish Soul Friends lived alongside Seekers and helped them make the best of life in body, mind, and spirit. Stories of Irish saints reveal different and endearing facets of Soul Friendship, which is seen as a gift that is especially precious during life's transitions.

EXERCISES

1. To find one's place of resurrection, first make a list of places that resonate with you. Number these in order of priority; the place that rings deepest and longest should be numbered one, and so on. Now pray about this place and see what natural links might develop. You may begin to sense that this place "is near but not quite it." Then keep on opening doors. Remember, your place of resurrection might be yours alone, so beware of jumping onto a bandwagon.

2. Make a list of your most prized friendships. Are you clutching, possessive, or jealous about any of these? Release your friends into God's hands, along with any persons to whom your friends are drawing closer. Pray for them to be built up in Christ.

Read More

Wisdom of the Celtic Saints by Edward Sellner (Ave Maria Press, 1993). The author presents the lives and teachings of twenty Celtic saints from the sixth to ninth centuries.

Stories of the Celtic Soul Friends: Their Meaning for Today by Edward Sellner (Paulist Press, 2004). This book includes stories of four leaders of the early Celtic church—Patrick, Brigit, Columcille, and Colman—to demonstrate the Soul Friend tradition's immediacy to our own faith and lives.

Notes

1. John Joseph Laux, ed. *The Life and Writings of Saint Columban* (Philadelphia, PA: Dolphin Press, 1914), p. 75.

2. John Ryan's *Irish Monasticism: Origins and Early Development* (Dublin, IE: Four Courts Press, 1992) gives extensive treatment of the training of monks and their roles within monasteries.

3. The sources for these stories in English translation are Whitley Stokes' *Lives of Saints from the Book of Lismore* (Burnham-on-Sea, UK: Llanerch, 1995) and Charles Plummer's *Lives of Irish Saints* (Oxford, UK: Oxford University Press, 1922).

4. Edward C. Sellner. *Mentoring: The Ministry of Spiritual Kindship* (Lanham, MD: Cowley Publications, 2002), p. 72.

5. Steve Maraboli. *Unapologetically You: Reflections on Life and the Human Experience* (Port Washington, NY: A Better Today, 2013).

6

Faithfulness

Insights from Soul Friends in Britain

(the fifth to seventh centuries after Christ)

The various accounts of holy men and women who lived in Britain[1] seldom use the Irish term Anamchara, yet they breathe a spirit of transparent friendship and deep spiritual counsel.

Ninian (Fifth Century): "Deservedly Was That Soul Called Friend"

Ninian apparently learned his Christian faith from his parents, who became followers of Christ during the Roman occupation of Britain. We have no information about any particular Soul Friend relationship, but we do learn from "The Miracles of Bishop Ninian," composed at Whithorn in the eighth century, that nobles and freemen entrusted the education of their sons to Ninian. He instructed them in knowledge, molded their characters, restrained vices with wholesome discipline, and instilled virtues. The anonymous author, no doubt a monk at the monastery Ninian founded at Whithorn, recounts that as Ninian was dying, Christ's voice called to him, addressing him as "my friend, my dove."

The author comments: "Deservedly was that soul called 'friend,' since it consisted entirely of love with no fear in it." So although we have few details, we sense that deep friendship, expressed in the spiritual formation of others, was integral to this foundational period of Christianity in Britain.

David and Brother Aidan (Sixth Century): "Of One Mind and Desire"

The eleventh-century biographer of David of Wales sometimes casts his praises of David in the mold of the Gospel accounts of Jesus. Like Jesus, who took his inner circle of three friends to the mountain or to the garden, David has an inner circle of three "most faithful disciples, namely Aidan, Eliud, and Ismael."[2] Of these three, Brother Aidan emerges as the one most akin to Jesus' beloved disciple John. The biographer describes David and Aidan as being "alike of one mind and desire," and the rapport between them transcended setback and separation, as the following episodes illustrate.

Friendship is one mind
in two bodies.

—MENCIUS

Aidan was outdoors studying one of the monastery's books, which had been painstakingly copied, when David asked him to go on an errand. This involved taking two oxen and a wagon to carry timber from some distance away. As always, Aidan was so eager to carry out errands in a good spirit that he promptly left, leaving his precious book still open. On his return journey, the wagon and oxen careened over a cliff. Aidan made the sign of the cross over them and retrieved them safely from the sea. Soon there was such a downpour that the ditches overflowed. Then Aidan thought of that precious book!

Having unloaded the timber, he went to retrieve the book, fearing the damage the downpour had done to it. However, he found the book in exactly the same condition as it was when he left it. The brothers who knew Aidan saw in this episode a link between an edifying Soul Friendship and the protecting hand of God. They felt that the humility and faith with which Aidan carried out the errand had provided a shield for the oxen in their fall, and that David's fatherly faith on behalf of his dear brother had provided a shield for the book.

Aidan's deep spiritual rapport with David continued even when he moved back to Ireland. He was praying in his monastery one Good Friday when he had an intimation that someone would poison David's food at their Easter Day supper in Wales. Aidan sent one of his monks, who with Divine guidance managed to cross the sea and reach David in time to warn him.

Rhigyfarch's *Life of St. David* tells us that the monks generally would reveal their thoughts to David. I have been to several Christian communities where brothers or sisters seem to flow together in mutual love. They have trust in their eyes and esteem in their hearts for one another, and they help each other in practical ways. That spirit marked David of Wales and his brothers, as these stories reveal.

Friendship
is a slow-ripening fruit.

—ARISTOTLE

Saint Aidan (Seventh Century): Loving Friendships with the English

OSWALD

Before King Oswald welcomed Bishop Aidan (who had no connection with Brother Aidan, friend of David) to his Northumbrian kingdom, Aidan was at the Iona monastery, where he would have been assigned an Irish Anamchara. After his move to Northumbria, Aidan himself had to be spiritual father to his eleven monks, to the Christ-followers around King Oswald's court, and to the new communities of Christians he hoped to establish in the area. To whom could he bare his own soul? I have sometimes wondered whether one of the eleven monks who were sent with him to Northumbria was an older man who acted as his confessor and spiritual father. We know that many more monks subsequently arrived from Ireland, perhaps some of them reviving links of friendship with Aidan. What is certain is that Aidan had a flare for developing new and deep spiritual friendships with both men and women, even though they were of a different ethnic group and language, and that these friendships bore great fruit.

Aidan also developed close friendships with succeeding kings. Can you imagine a king of a warrior race not only being willing to act as an interpreter among poor villagers as did Oswald (because no one else was at first available to interpret Aidan's Irish dialect), but also being willing to walk with Aidan rather than ride a royal horse? This could only have happened because there was a profound bond of trust and friendship between Aidan and Oswald.

OSWIN

Oswald's successor, King Oswin, gave Aidan the gift of a royal horse—and Aidan gave the horse away to a passing beggar. Oswin's reaction indicates that these two men also had a Soul Friendship. Bede informs us that Oswin was tall, handsome, courteous, and beloved by all. The king, who had reprimanded Aidan for giving away such a horse, then accepted Aidan's reprimand: "Is that son of a mare more precious to you than that son of God?" He received Aidan's words deep into his soul. After a time of reflection, he knelt before Aidan in contrition and promised never again to interfere with Aidan's ministry. Aidan was so moved that a king could be so humble, such a man after God's own heart, that he had a premonition that brought tears to his eyes. He perceived that Oswin's lack of warlikeness would bring his imminent defeat and death in war. This indeed happened. Some scholars believe that Aidan's own unexpected death only eleven days after Oswin's was brought on by a broken heart. Soul friendship indeed!

HILDA

No doubt Aidan was introduced to Hilda through Oswald, who was a relative. Aidan heard that Hilda, who had gone to reside with relatives in the court of East Anglia, had decided to become a nun and join her sister for novice training at the French monastery of Chelles. Aidan pleaded with her to help develop the monastic life in her own kingdom. Hilda agreed, and Aidan seems to have offered her a personalized form of training. Bede informs us that Aidan, along with other devout men who had gotten to know Hilda, "visited her frequently, instructed her assiduously, and loved her heartily for her innate wisdom and her devotion to the service of God."[3] Hilda herself become a spiritual mother to many people, and Bede tells us that ordinary people and rulers sought her counsel.

Cuthbert and Boisil (Seventh Century): "He Knew Everything About Him"

The anonymous monk of Lindisfarne who wrote the earliest life of Cuthbert fitted the experiences of Cuthbert into the pattern established by the authors of two lives: "The Life of St. Antony," ascribed to Athanasius and made available in Northumbria in the Latin translation of Evagrius, and "The Life of St. Martin of Tours" by Sulpicius Severus. It is likely that Cuthbert himself, as well as his fellow monk and biographer, allowed the desert and ascetic tradition to shape his life, not least in the value it placed upon spiritual fathers and mothers.[4]

"The Anonymous Life of Cuthbert" seems to have been written within twenty years of Cuthbert's death in 687. The author was able to draw on the recollections of several people who had a particularly close friendship with Cuthbert: the priest Plegcils; the nun Kenswith, who had been Cuthbert's foster mother; and Prior Aethilwald of Melrose. Either the Lindisfarne monk or Bede, who added to this account, also wrote down recollections of people who had known of other close friendships in Cuthbert's life. Each recollection has a distinctive hue, such as those with Boisil, the prophetic prior; Herbert, the Cumbrian hermit; and Herefrith, the spiritual father at Lindisfarne at the time of Cuthbert's dying.

While Cuthbert was guarding sheep on the Lammermuir hills one night in 651, when he was seventeen, he saw a vision of Aidan being taken to heaven. The next day, he rode with his servant to Melrose monastery and offered himself for monastic service to the prior, Boisil. Since it was Cuthbert's vision of the death of Lindisfarne's Aidan that led him to so dedicate himself, why did he choose Melrose rather than Lindisfarne? According to Bede, it was because Cuthbert was attracted by Boisil's reputation as a wise teacher and guide.

As soon as Cuthbert and Boisil met, there seems to have been a rapport between them; each recognized the high calling of the other. As Boisil saw the way Cuthbert dismounted from his horse and bade farewell to his servant, to his horse, and to the sword he had handed to his servant, he said to his companion: "You are looking at a true servant of God." Bede suggests that it brought to mind Jesus' assessment of Nathaniel: "Here is a true Israelite, a person without guile" (John 1:47).

Boisil took Cuthbert as his pupil and taught him a deep love of the Gospels, especially John. Bede, in his "Prose Life of St. Cuthbert," records these words of Cuthbert: "In Boisil's old age, when I was but a youth, he brought me up in the monastery at Melrose and amid his instructions predicted with prophetic truth all the things which were to happen to me."

For some years Cuthbert was away from Boisil at the Ripon monastery where he was guest master. After his return to Melrose, Cuthbert "most diligently paid heed to both the words and deeds of Boisil as he had before."

Soon, there was an outbreak of the plague. Cuthbert himself caught it, but he recovered; then Boisil succumbed. Boisil asked Cuthbert to be with him and spoke to him in a prophetic way: "You will not get the plague a second time, but I will die of it." At the time, Herefrith, a priest at Lindisfarne and later abbot there, was in the monastery. He told Bede how, in the last week of his life, Boisil proposed to spend his time teaching his disciple:

> Cuthbert asked, "And what is best for me to read that I can finish in one week?"
>
> Boisil replied, "The evangelist John. I have a book consisting of seven sections; with the Lord's help we can get through one every day, reading it and discussing it so far as is necessary."

Bede saw significance in the way the two men read the Scriptures together: "They dealt with the simple things of 'the faith that works by love'" (Galatians 5:6). Love was the key to John's friendship with Jesus, and it was the key to Boisil's friendship with Cuthbert.

Boisil shared the accumulated wisdom of his heart and his head with his disciple. During those last seven days of reading and sharing, Boisil also "declared all Cuthbert's future to him." Boisil's prophetic prayers for Cuthbert came out of their reflections upon the Scriptures and out of their love for one another. It is not too often that a friendship combines such a rapport with such a prophetic edge; when it does, it is something we should prize, as Cuthbert prized his friendship with Boisil.

Bede's summary of Cuthbert's life is that he received from Boisil "a knowledge of the Scriptures and the example of a life of good works." A knowledge of holy Scriptures and an example of a good life form foundations of Soul Friendship that last.

> Now Cuthbert had
> great numbers of people
> coming to him
> not just from Lindisfarne
> but even from the
> remote parts of Britain. . . .
> They confessed their sins,
> confided in him
> about their temptations
> and laid open to him
> the common troubles
> of humanity they were

> labouring under—
> all in the hope of
> gaining consolation
> from so holy a man.
>
> —BEDE

CUTHBERT AS A SOUL FRIEND

Cuthbert drew deeply from his own spiritual guides and became a spiritual guide to others, at first as a busy pastor, and later as a hermit. When he became prior of Melrose, he sometimes went away for a month offering pastoral care to people even in the most inaccessible villages. From Melrose, he was transferred to be prior of Lindisfarne. Bede says that there he continued the practical "works of mercy" that he had displayed at Melrose, and his reputation as a holy man who ministered to people's bodily and spiritual ailments in the power of God continued to grow. It's no wonder that when he withdrew to the solitary Farne Isle for nine years, great numbers of penitents and pilgrims, even from remote parts of Britain, followed him there to seek his guidance. Bede writes of Cuthbert:

> No one left uncomforted, no one had to carry back the burdens they brought with them. With a

word from God he would rekindle spirits that were chilled by sorrow. He brought back to the joys of heaven those weighed down with worry. . . . To people beset with temptation he would skillfully disclose the ploys of the devil, explaining that a person who lacks love for God or others is easily caught in the devil's traps, while a person strong in faith can, with God's help, brush them aside like so many spiders' webs.

A house was built where those who made the crossing could wait to meet Cuthbert. In due course, Cuthbert would come and give each visitor counsel and prayer. Cuthbert was continuing the tradition of the Fathers of the Desert who were sought out as spiritual guides.

Although the accounts of Cuthbert's life give sparse details, we can glean that certain people used Cuthbert as a spiritual guide over a long period. This is in addition to the villagers to whom Cuthbert gave pastoral care and the visitors to Farne Isle who sought guidance.

No one can displease me
by waking me out of my sleep,
but, on the contrary,

> give me pleasure;
> for, by rousing me
> from inactivity, he
> enables me to do or think
> of something useful.
>
> —CUTHBERT

Kenswith, the first nun in Northumbria whose name we know, was asked to be Cuthbert's foster mother when he was a boy. It seems that the Saxons who embraced Christianity also embraced the custom of the Irish Christians who evangelized them in providing holy foster mothers for children. Kenswith outlived Cuthbert, but Cuthbert may have outgrown her in discernment as well as in learning. We learn from Bede's account of a fire that broke out in her village while Cuthbert was there that he maintained visits to his foster mother as an adult, and that she immediately turned to him for help.

HERMIT BONDS BETWEEN CUTHBERT AND HERBERT

Herbert was a hermit priest on an island in Derwentwater, who, Bede tells us, "had long been bound to Cuthbert . . . by the bonds of spiritual friendship." During Cuthbert's years at Lindisfarne and Farne, Herbert walked across the land each year to spend time with him. After Cuthbert became chief pastor of the Northumbrians, he made plans for a pastoral visit to Carlisle. Herbert decided to make Carlisle the venue for his annual visit with his friend. Bede pictures Herbert hoping to be inspired to heavenly desires by Cuthbert, and the two of them "refreshing each other with draughts of living waters."

Herbert stayed overnight with Cuthbert as a fellow guest. During their time together, Cuthbert said, "Remember to ask me now whatever you need to know and to discuss with me, for I am sure this is the last time we shall meet in this life, and that I shall soon move into the next life."

Herbert wept. On his knees, he pleaded with Cuthbert: "Remember your most faithful companion, and ask the Lord in his mercy that as we have served him together on earth, so we may journey together with him to heaven. For you know that I have always tried to live my life in accordance with your guidance, and when I have gone the wrong way through ignorance or frailty, I have always tried to put things right according to your advice."

Cuthbert went aside to pray through this, and God gave him the assurance that he would grant this request. Events confirmed this witness in Cuthbert's spirit. They never saw each other again. Herbert underwent a long illness, and they both went to heaven on March 20 of the same year.

The Soul Friendships explored in this chapter have two things in common: community and faithfulness. The wisdom of these Soul Friends grew in relationship to a community of which they remained part, even when, like Cuthbert and Herbert, they were called away to the solitary life. Spiritual guides who divorce themselves from the community of Christ's Body may lack that wholeness of understanding and feeling that is the heart of true Soul Friendship. It was the stability of community that enabled these Soul Friends to remain faithful through the vicissitudes of the years.

Hermit Soul Friendships continue today. For example, Brother Harold, hermit of Shepherd's Law, Northumberland, travels each winter to Southern France to spend time with his hermit Soul Friend there.

Christians in ordinary life, when they seek a Soul Friend, continue to turn to members of religious orders. Sometimes they seek out those who have dedicated themselves in greater or lesser degree to a hermit life. In order to find the necessary solitude, some of these Soul Friends live in places difficult to access. Like Herbert and Cuthbert, the visits become fewer but longer.

Summary

The thread that runs through most of the accounts of these saints is the faithfulness they showed in their friendships and counsel. Without this faithfulness, we may question whether Hilda would have made Britain her mission field, whether the Irish-British fellowship would have survived, and whether hermits would have died with such peace.

EXERCISES

For Soul Friends and Seekers
to do together or separately.

1. At Eastertide, Brother Aidan's thoughts turned to his old Soul Friend David. Use a time of vigil to recall and bless those who have helped you in times past.

2. Hilda might have been lost to the Christian mission in Britain were it not for Aidan's friendship and belief in her. Pray for your friends, imagining how God sees and wants to use their potential.

3. Cuthbert gained from Boisil a knowledge of the Scriptures and the example of a life of good works. Review your life. How can you gain a more complete knowledge of the Scriptures? Are there good works which you have yet to do?

Read More

Aidan, Bede, Cuthbert: Three Inspirational Saints by David Adam (SPCK, 2006). The author demonstrates that these men have much to teach us about expanding our spiritual awareness and deepening our love for God.

You might also enjoy my *St Aidan's Way of Mission: Celtic Insights for a Post-Christian World* (Bible Reading Fellowship, 2016).

Notes

1. Ninian and David were Britons; Brother Aidan and Saint Aidan of Lindisfarne were Irish who lived in Britain; Cuthbert, Herbert, Hilda, Oswald, and Oswin were Saxons, and Boisil might have been any of these.

2. Rhigyfarch. *Life of St. David,* translated by J. W. James (Cardiff, UK: University of Wales Press, 1967), ch. 15.

3. Bede. *The Ecclesiastical History of the English People*, translated by Bertram Colgrave and R.A.B. Mynors (Oxford, UK: Oxford University Press, 1994), p. 1V 23.

4. The four sources I have drawn on in this chapter are: *The Life of St. Cuthbert* by an anonymous monk of Lindisfarne available in *Two Lives of St. Cuthbert*, edited and translated by Bertram Colgrave. (Cambridge, UK: Cambridge University Press, 1985); Bede's *Life of St. Cuthbert,* now available

in the above and in *The Age of Bede*, translated by J.F. Webb and D.H. Farmer (New York, NY: Penguin, 1985); *Bede's Metrical Life of St. Cuthbert*, now available in *Cuthbert, His Cult and Community*, edited by G. Bonner et al. (Haworth, NJ: Woodbridge, 1989); and *Bede's Ecclesiastical History of the English People*, edited and translated by Bertram Colgrave and R.A.B. Mynors (Oxford, UK: Oxford University Press, 1994).

7
Wildness

Pilgrim Insights into Soul Friendship

(the fifth to sixth centuries after Christ)

Celtic Christians who journeyed to wild places were sought out as Soul Friends. They also became icons for the Soul Friends and Seekers who stayed at home, but who recognized that life's journey needs to go beyond comfort zones.

Celtic Christians who ventured across land or sea to seek God in wild places were admired as "white martyrs," because their long, dangerous pilgrimages required a letting-go and a self-giving second only to physical martyrdom. The stories of Brendan's hair-raising adventures on the ocean (in the fifth to sixth centuries), of Samson's victories against serpent or wild wolf (also in the fifth to sixth centuries), of hermits confronting elements and demons on rocky outposts—these spurred those who heard them to seek God's next steps for their own lives. These "pilgrims for the love of God" became models for the majority who did not travel, but who did not want to get stuck in a rut.

In the Bible, the Hebrew and Greek words sometimes translated as "desert" are also translated as "wilderness," and this word is often used in classic descriptions of the spiritual journey. The scriptural wilderness is a place of testing that ultimately leads to an encounter with God. This reminds us that we are called to face the wild places in our lives and harness these as channels for the Divine presence. To know God means that no part of life is kept in a separate compartment. It was surely not for nothing that the Bible translators came to use the word "wilderness." None of us goes for long without some wilderness that we need to traverse.

Celtic theologian John Scotus Eriugena perceived the movement of God's Spirit in creation (Genesis 1:1,2) as a turbulent swirl of the four elements, a wildness of energy that gives rise to creativity. The Spirit can move through the turbulent waters of our lives. The focus of spiritual direction in the Celtic tradition lies less in helping a Seeker to conform to norms of convention than in helping a Seeker to be true to the wild movements of the Spirit that transcend convention.

*In God's wildness
lies the hope
of the world.*

—JOHN MUIR

I once asked someone, "What draws you to follow the Way of Life of the Community of Aidan and Hilda?"

"There is a wild man somewhere inside me waiting to get out," he replied. "The Celtic Christians knew how to move out of their safety zones. They had no forbidden areas for God."

Soul Friends in the Celtic tradition never encourage Seekers to hide from their wild inner spirits, but to acknowledge them and harness them to the Great Spirit. In this chapter, we shall allow some outstanding wild and holy wanderers to teach us.

In their own way, these long-ago Celtic Christians were following the example of ancient Hebrew believers, of Jesus himself, and of the spiritual Fathers and Mothers of Egypt, who all journeyed into deserts. Columba's biographer, Adamnan, tells the story of Cormac's dangerous voyage north to find a "desert in the sea" (in the sixth or seventh century). Columba revealed that in his desire to reach this "desert," Cormac, had to voyage three times through stormy waters.

Michael, the most popular angelic being in the Hebrides, is said to ride a white unharnessed horse with a sword of elemental flame to combat the dragon. He does not attempt to subdue the wind, nor does he domesticate the wild horse. The dragon represents the destructive potential, while the wind and the wild horse represent the creative potential in elemental forces. In spiritual direction, we learn to embrace and harness the good in the wildness in order to master the destructive in it.

Carl Jung helped twentieth-century folk understand that the psyche of Western people has a wilderness. He wrote that the undercurrents of the psychic life of the West are uninviting. We have slaved away to build a monumental world around us, but it is only imposing because we have lavished all that is imposing in our natures on the outside, and we have left what is shabby on the inside. He says it is necessary—even though it is hard—to look into the psychic depths, because it is only there we will find the creative currents for something new:

> At first we cannot
> see beyond the path
> that leads downward
> to dark and hateful things—
> but no light or beauty
> will ever come from the
> person who cannot bear this sight.
> Light is always born of darkness,
> and the sun never yet stood still
> in heaven to satisfy
> person's longings
> or to still their fears.
>
> —CARL JUNG[1]

Each of us has to journey beyond our comfort zones, into those wild and untrodden places within ourselves—if not in physically distant places—that beckon to us. This requires us to let go of the control patterns that we impose upon our lives, and to become open to what lies beyond. To do this we need guides along the way.

Ciaran of Saigir (Sixth Century): Ireland's John the Baptist

Ciaran of Saigir, who was known as "the firstborn of the saints of Ireland," became an early model of the holy wild wanderer. He was born on Clear Island off the coast of Cork, the southernmost point of Ireland. Since he was clad in skins and lived in caves with wild animals, biographers cast him in the role of Ireland's John the Baptist, preparing the way for Saint Patrick's mission.

A wild boar and a wolf became his first "monks" at Saigir. Then, according to "The Litany of Pilgrim Saints," fifteen people went with Ciaran to Scotland. The ruin of a medieval chapel on the Rhinns of Islay is probably the site of Ciaran's cell. His voyage to Scotland became the first to capture the popular imagination.[2]

Celtic hermits deliberately chose to live lives exposed to the elements. They called God "Lord of the Elements," and they sensed that the elements of Nature mirror raw elements in our own natures. By exposing themselves to the one, they got in touch with the other.

E. G. Bowen[3] charts the journeys of many of these wandering pilgrims, known as *peregrini*. Some went along the western seaways from Sutherland to Finistere. Others went to the warmer lands of the south, but most ventured into the dark and stormy waters of the north, reaching the Orkneys,

Shetlands, the Faroes, and even Iceland. The heroic voyages of the few became archetypes of the inner journeys of many.

A friend is a loved one
who awakens your life
in order to free
the wild possibilities within you.

—JOHN O'DONOHUE[4]

Saint Kevin (Sixth Century): Our Hidden Monsters

In their book *Glendalough: A Celtic Pilgrimage*, authors Michael Rodgers and Marcus Losack portray the experience of Kevin, Glendalough's "hermit of the wild," as an image of our own inner journey.[5] For them, the stories of Kevin suggest his life was driven not only by a desire for solitude but also to reach for the edges of life.

Kevin was a wild man clothed in animal skins. He is said to have prayed for one hour every night in the cold waters of the lake where a monster used to distract and annoy him by curling itself around his body, biting and stinging him. In another story, he banished a monster from the Lower Lake to the Upper Lake. As Kevin lived alone at the Upper Lake, in effect he took the monster to himself. It was said that the fervor of his prayer, his patience, and God's love in him rendered the monster harmless.

Rodgers and Losack write:

> The story of the monster in the lake is revealing in the light of modern psychology's understanding of the unconscious mind which can have such an impact on our behavior and responses. It has been said that the history of monsters is the history of humanity's struggle to see its own inner face. Certainly there lurks in all of us "a little monster" that tends to push down deep inside us in one way or another.
>
> What happens when we consign our dark thoughts into the deep waters of our mind? Do they not tend to re-emerge in "monstrous" form, perhaps even as the "monsters" we see in others? What did Kevin do? It appears that he moved the monster to the Upper Lake where he himself lived.

It might be said that he acknowledged its presence and tried to befriend it. Perhaps there is a key in that story for each of us.

Kevin lived in a small cave, now known as St. Kevin's Bed, fifty feet above the lake. He chose to live on the side of the lake that is in shade for a full six months every year. His decision to go to this dark and inhospitable place seems to lie at the heart of the Glendalough experience. After Kevin's death and out of this experience, a significant monastic city grew there.

Why did Kevin do this? Perhaps he needed to stretch himself to the limit—to go to the very edge—in order to get to that place of total, childlike dependence upon God. He needed to experience the innocence of the first human beings, who like Kevin were clothed in skins and walked naked and alone with God in the shade of a primitive garden. Kevin's Bed challenges us to enter our place of vulnerability and fear.

Go to the place
of your greatest fear
and there you will find
your greatest strength.

—ANONYMOUS

Accompanying a Seeker Through Wild Places

Inquirers who ask the Community of Aidan and Hilda if they can test out its way with a Soul Friend for a trial period are known as Explorers. The next step, the making of first promises, is known as Making the First Voyage of the Coracle.[5] A member of the Community welcomes them with these words:

> Brothers and sisters, God is calling you to leave behind everything that stops you setting sail in the ocean of God's love. You have heard the call of the Wild Goose, the untamable Spirit of God: be ready for him to lead you into wild, windy or well-worn places in the knowledge that he will make them places of wonder and welcome.

Richard Rohr, the co-author of the book *The Wild Man's Journey*,[6] had to go to India to find a culture where the concept of the wild man is generally understood. He discovered that Indians traditionally divide a person's life into four stages: the student, the householder, the seeker, and the wise person. The third stage, regarded in the West as a time of householding and business that is the main focus of life, is viewed by Indians as merely a transition stage. They sometimes refer to the seeker as a forest dweller; he does not necessarily go off to the woods, but he goes off alone to explore the meaning of life. "After years of having experienced life," Rohr writes, "they are now in a position to begin to understand it, to look for the big picture." Compared with this, Rohr claims, the Western view of life is shortsighted and pleasure-centered; and Westerners do not expect old people to journey into wisdom in the fourth stage of old age.

As Soul Friends, how do we apply this aspect of life to a person who spends her life amid the dull routines of an office-bound city? The role of a Soul Friend is to discern if and when the time is right to point the Seeker toward this kind of journey. The Seeker will know when she is ready, and the Soul Friend must respect her choice. On the one hand, never try to push; on the other hand, never try to hold back the Seeker.

For example, if the Seeker is in a dark place, journey with her into this, rather than try to find an escape route or give pat answers to agonized questions. Or perhaps the Seeker is coming near to a place of anger. Listen to the Seeker and sympathize. If appropriate, look at temporary ways of coping, but do not let attention to symptoms deflect the Seeker from going deeper into the things that feed the anger. Likewise, a Soul Friend will try to find out what is the fear behind a fear.

> A Soul Friend may repeat
> this prayer for a Seeker:
>
> Wild Spirit of the Almighty,
> Be your eye in the dark places.
> Be your flight in the trapped places.
> Be your host in the wild places.
> Be your brood in the barren places.
> Be your formation in the lost places.

What if the Soul Friend feels out of his depth? He can respond in one of three ways: give up; realize that, though he has not traveled where the Seeker is now traveling, he doesn't need to be intimidated by this because he has traveled to other places; or learn to travel humbly alongside the Seeker. The Soul Friend can also pray for the Seeker—for release from entanglement in false inner networks of negativity; for confidence; for movement toward the paths that attract the Seeker.

Summary

A good Soul Friend will encourage the Seeker to explore the "wild places" of her life. God can be encountered in deeper ways and new wisdom and insight gained in these unexplored, challenging areas.

EXERCISES

For Soul Friends and Seekers

1. What apron strings still exist in your life? To what or to whom are you clinging?

2. How far have you journeyed into your creativity? What might it mean to do this?

3. How far have you journeyed (if you are female) into the masculine side of your nature, or (if you are male) into the feminine side?

4. What areas of emotional pain do you try to avoid?

5. What is the place of your greatest fear? If you are not sure, jot down fears you become aware of during the days and during the nights. What do these tell you? What might your fears have to teach you?

6. What about a journey into responsibility? What areas of life have you abdicated from?

7. What are the monsters in your life, the "destroyers of life" that you need to confront and conquer?

8. Saint Brendan sailed in search of "Paradise Island." What are your unrealized God-given hopes?

Read More

The Wild Land Within: Cultivating Wholeness through Spiritual Practice by Lisa Colón DeLay (Broadleaf, 2021). Through spiritual practices from desert monastics, as well as Latinx, Black, and indigenous contemplatives, the author offers a guide to encountering a God of wildness and mystery.

Notes

1. C.G. Jung. *Modern Man In Search of a Soul* (New York, NY: Routledge & Kegan Paul, 1978), p. 248.

2. See John Marsden's *Sea-Road of the Saints: Celtic Holy Men in the Hebrides* (Edinburgh, UK: Floris, 1995).

3. E.G. Bowen. *Saints, Seaways, and Settlements in the Celtic Lands* (Cardiff, UK: University of Wales Press, 1977).

4. John O'Donohue. *Anam Cara: A Book of Celtic Wisdom* (New York, NY: HarperCollins, 2009), p. 19.

5. Michael Rodgers and Marcus Losack. *Glendalough: A Celtic Pilgrimage* (Dublin, IE: The Columba Press 1996).

6. *The First Voyage of the Coracle with The Way of Life*, Community of Aidan and Hilda, Lindisfarne Retreat, Holy Island, Berwick Upon Tweed, TD15 2SD.

7. Richard Rohr and Joseph Martos. *The Wild Man's Journey: Reflections on Male Spirituality* (Cincinnati, OH: St. Anthony Messenger Press, 1991), ch. 16.

8

Prophecy

Columba's and Ciaran's Insights into Soul Friendship

(the sixth century after Christ)

he Irish have a tradition they call *soul-making*—reviewing the direction of one's life, having the courage to change, and seeking to relate harmoniously to the physical and the spiritual environment. The link between prophecy and Soul Friendship, which is necessary to this process, is seen clearly in Columba, as Adamnan's "Life" illustrates.[1]

Columba (521–597) had the benefit of an upbringing in one of Ireland's ruling families, and as a young Christ-follower, he chose Ireland's best mentors to lead him in different aspects of the Way. First, he journeyed far from his home in Donegal, to study at Moville under Finnian, who had acquired knowledge in the magnificent library at Ninian's Whithorn. Next, Columba traveled south to Leinster to draw from the bard Gemman the wisdom of poetry, folk memory, and the creative flow that facilitates Christ-centered identity. Then, to fulfill a need for mentoring of a different sort, Columba moved to the renowned monastery at Clonard. There, under another Finnian, he became immersed in the spirituality of the early fathers of the church; and through the writings of Cassian, he studied the Fathers and Mothers of the Eastern deserts. He would also have learned to network with the church in Wales, where Finnian had been trained.

Countless people soon sought out Columba as a Soul Friend. Most of them traveled a long way to seek his advice, then moved on in their life journey, keeping only occasional contact through the years. A few remained Soul Friends for life. The reason for this pattern was partly Columba's stature as overseer of his large family of churches, but partly his clear perception of an individual's future path. The story of Libran illustrates the link between prophecy and individual care.

Purity, wisdom
and prophecy,
These are the gifts
I would ask of Thee;
O High King of Heaven,
grant them to me.

—COLUMBA'S PRAYER
FROM THE PLAY *COLUMBA*

Columba and Libran

A farmworker (later named Libran) in Connaught, Ireland, committed a crime of passion; he killed a man. While he was in prison under sentence of death, a wealthy relative paid a large ransom fee, in return for Libran's promise to work as his slave for the rest of his life. After a few days as a slave, Libran escaped and went on a long journey to make penance for his crime. Arriving at Columba's island monastery at Iona, Libran asked Columba to accept him as a novice monk. Columba put him through a rigorous appraisal, explaining that if someone was not truly called to the monastic life, the duties would be too much to bear. Kneeling before Columba, Libran made a full confession of his sins and dedicated himself to do anything or go anywhere under Columba's direction. The obedience he had refused to his relative, he now willingly gave to Columba.

God flashed into Columba's mind what Libran was called to do. He was to serve in Columba's Mag Luinge monastery at Tiree for seven years, refraining from certain meals and from Holy Communion as a penance. Following this probationary period, he was to return to Iona for Lent. This he did. Following the penances of Lent, he was welcomed back into the full fellowship of the church and received the sacrament with joy at the Easter celebration.

Inwardly, however, Libran was still agonizing over the oath he had failed to keep with his relative more than seven years before, so he asked to talk this through with Columba. Once again, God put into Columba's mind what lay ahead for Libran.

"Your former master and your father, your mother, and your brothers are still alive," Columba told him. "You must prepare yourself for a long voyage." Columba then gave Libran a ceremonial sword, which was a mark of the bond between a ruler and his subject. "Take this as a gift you can offer your master in return for your freedom. He has a wife with many virtues; he will take her advice, and release you there and then without demanding any fee."

A serious sin can lead to one tangle after another. Life is not as simple as we would like, nor was it for Libran. By going to prison and then escaping, Libran had neglected the service due from a son to his father. This had caused resentment in his brothers. Columba intuitively understood all this and was given prophetic guidance to deal with this second tangle. Columba informed Libran that although he would be released from the first obligation about which he was so anxious, he would not be released from his family obligations. Columba told Libran that his brothers would force him to make good the service he owed to his father.

This was Columba's advice, combined with a reassuring prophecy: "Obey your brothers without hesitation, and take your old father into your care. Although this will seem a heavy burden, it will not be for long, for one week after you begin the care of your father he will die. Your brothers will press you to take on the care of your mother, but your younger brother will volunteer to take your place."

All this came true. The wife of Libran's former master told her husband: "Holy Columba's blessing will do us more good than this gift, so release this man to Columba without payment." Libran then undertook to care for his father, but the old man died only a week later, just as Columba had foretold. And when Libran's brothers demanded that he stay to look after their mother, the younger brother spoke up: "Our brother has spent the last seven years working for the salvation of his soul with Columba in Britain; it is not right that we should hold him back."

So Libran made his farewells and tried to board a boat that was leaving Derry to take him to Scotland. The help of his Soul Friend was needed even at this distance, however, for the sailors refused to let him on board. Libran started to talk to Columba as if he were physically present.

"I bet you are not pleased that these men have full sails and a fair wind but they won't take me," he said loudly to Columba. At that the wind changed, the boat slowed, and Libran ran beside it. The men, who probably heard Libran's words, started to discuss whether the wind might change again in their favor if they took him with them.

"The prayers of Columba, with whom I have spent seven years, will be able to get you a fair wind," Libran told them. They took him on board. Libran, conscious of Columba's unseen support, prayed in the name of Almighty God, and the winds took them to their destination.

When Libran reached Iona, it was not he but Columba who related everything that had happened. Libran was permitted to take full monastic vows, and that was the occasion when Columba gave him the name by which we know him, Libran, because he had been so truly liberated.

Columba sent Libran back to the Tiree monastery with this prophetic blessing: "You will enjoy life long into old age.

Nevertheless, your place of resurrection will be in Ireland, not Britain."

This made Libran weep, so Columba comforted him with these words: "You need have no distress. You will die in one of my monasteries and you will have your share in the kingdom among my specially chosen monks. You will wake from death into the resurrection of eternal life with them."

Libran was comforted, indeed enriched, by this blessing and went away at peace. After working many years in the reed beds of the monastery at Tiree, and after Columba himself had passed into heaven, an ancient Libran was sent to the Columban monastery of Durrow, Ireland, on some community business. He became ill, died, and was buried there in peace.

Without Columba's prophetic support, Libran would never have had the assurance he needed to go and do right by his former master and by his family. If this unfinished business had not been dealt with, he would have lacked the inner healing that enabled him to live such a long and fruitful life.

Columba was not alone among Soul Friends in his use of prophetic gifts. Though few are given foreknowledge in such detail as was he, more people are given mental pictures that carry a vision for another. Such were the prophetic visions that guided Ciaran.

O Lord, grant us that love
which can never die,
which will enkindle our lamps
but not extinguish them,
so that they may shine in us
and bring light to others.
Most dear Savior,
enkindle our lamps
that they may shine
forever in your temple.
May we receive
unquenchable light from you
so that our darkness
will be illuminated
and the darkness of the world
will be made less.
Amen.

—COLUMBA

Ciaran (512–545) and the Prophecy of the Spreading Tree

In the sixth century, young people with a sense of vocation went to the island of Aran to study under Enda, the most famous teacher in Ireland. Some sought the advice of this monastic leader, and others sought after a Soul Friend. Ciaran, an anointed young leader who was searching for God's next steps for him, was one of those who flocked to Aran. During Ciaran's period of study there, both he and Enda had a similar vision.

A large and fruitful tree grew beside a river in the middle of Ireland. The tree protected the entire island, its fruit crossed the sea, and the birds carried off some of its fruit to the world. Enda then interpreted the vision to Ciaran: "The tree is you. All Ireland will be sheltered by your grace and many people will be fed by your fasting and prayers. In the name of God, go to the center of Ireland and found your church on the banks of a river."

As a result of this guidance, Ciaran founded the monastery of Clonmacnoise, which was a major influence for a thousand years, and whose ruins still evoke awe today.

Soul Friendship and Prophecy

The purpose of prophecy is to build up people and release them into their destiny. Few of us may be given Columba's frequency and clarity of prophecy, but many of us are given what is needed for a particular person or situation.

A Soul Friend should not be shy to ask a Seeker if he would like a time of silent prayer, during which the Soul Friend and the Seeker share any pictures or Scriptures that come into their minds that they feel may be from God. Many of us may fear to do this, not out of embarrassment, but in case we get it wrong. We have a healthy fear of brainwashing, and we do not wish a Seeker to do something that is not right for her. There is no need, however, to let this fear discourage prophetic prayer. We can simply offer what we feel God has put into our minds, and make clear that the Seeker should weigh this, as Saint Paul says we should with any prophecy (1 Corinthians 14:29). If both the Soul Friend and the Seeker have a sense of peace and rightness about something that is shared, it is best to move ahead in the light of it, though still keeping open the possibility that God may have to correct distortions.

We do need to beware of giving people what pleases their ego. In his book *Soul Friend,* Kenneth Leech recalls a critique that R.A. Lambourne made of the pastoral counseling movement in the 1960s: "There was an excessive preoccupation with self-development at the expense of justice and matter."[2] In contrast, Leech cites Thomas Merton's view that a spiritual guide must question the fundamental values of society.

Sometimes a conviction will come to a Soul Friend that feels as if it is not his own insight; it is "pure gift." Perhaps he is quaking with this conviction, or a picture or a word flashed through his mind, and it seems as if God has directly given him something for the Seeker. As with all prophetic messages, this needs to be weighed, so it should be offered humbly, in a provisional way. It is wise for the Soul Friend to say to the Seeker that he may have gotten it wrong—but it is worth offering it nonetheless. The Seeker can then be included in the process of discussing and interpreting it, and this can be creative. Such input can sometimes give the Seeker a motivation that was previously lacking; sometimes it can break through a mental log-jam, or it can open up a new process or a new direction.

Summary

The purpose of using prophecy in Soul Friendships is to free a Seeker from acquiescence to a comfortable or defensive status quo, so that she may travel the road God has for her. Soul Friends who lack the precision of Columba's vision may still offer what they do see, drawing out the Seeker until she sees it for herself, or at least sharing it for the Seeker to weigh.

EXERCISES

1. Columba recognized that Libran could not go forward until he had dealt with the unfinished business in his past life. Take time to write down any unfinished business in your life; then ask God to show you how you should deal with it.

2. If you are a Soul Friend, invite God to give you a picture for the Seeker(s) for whom you pray.

Read More

Life of St. Columba by Adamnan, edited and translated with extensive footnotes by Richard Sharpe (Penguin, 1995). A third of this book is a record of Columba's prophecies to friends.

Notes

1. The material on Columba in this chapter is taken from Adamnan's *Life of St. Columba,* translated by Richard Sharpe (New York, NY: Penguin, 1995).
2. Kenneth Leech. *Soul Friend* (New York, NY: Morehouse, 2001).

9

Fitness Training

Columbanus's Insights into Soul Friendship

(the sixth and seventh centuries after Christ)

Penance, which seems bizarre to most modern minds, was really fitness training. It was the means of becoming fit for a destiny in an eternal realm. Those who led the way in this were known as athletes of the Spirit. The leaders of many Celtic Christian communities wrote out fitness-training programs not only for their members but also for those in the general public who looked to the communities for guidance. These were known as *Penitentials.*

On the continent, a person might confess his sins to a priest he hardly knew, who would declare that he was forgiven without having to make restitution to anyone he had wronged. The priest might suggest an act of self-discipline that was often perfunctory and rarely increased real self-mastery. Penitentials produced by Celtic leaders were more far-reaching, however. Along with David of Britain, Columbanus was a frontrunner in this area, and his rigorous fitness-training programs influenced many people, including local bishops who sought Columbanus as a spiritual guide.[1] Soul Friends today will not want to copy the details found in these ancient fitness manuals, but they can nevertheless use many of the principles in their work with Seekers.

In the Celtic tradition, penance is thought of in a positive light, as making an act of dedication for love of God, in order to overcome and leave behind the things that have hindered that love. The person making an act of penance is like a lover saying to her beloved: "I give you the gift beyond price—myself, all of me, always. To help me to do this—and so you can have no doubts—I will visibly leave behind all counter attractions to you, and accompany only you. In this way, you will know at all times that you alone are the love of my life." In this light, penance becomes something beautiful.

*The beauty of the fish
in his bright lake;
beautiful too its surface
shimmering.
The beauty of the word
with which the Trinity speaks;
beautiful too doing
penance for sin.*

—THE LOVES OF TALIESIN[2]

In one Penitential, Columbanus explained that just as doctors use different medicines to treat bodily ailments, so spiritual doctors should use different cures for the various wounds of the soul. He acknowledged that few of us have the gift of being a spiritual doctor, so he set out "a few prescriptions according to the traditions of our elders, and according to our own partial understanding."

These prescriptions focused on eight principal vices that damage our ability to be effective human beings: gluttony, avarice, rage, self-pity, lust, slackness, vanity, and pride. The vices had to be healed by taking their opposite virtues, like medicine. The principle was cure by contraries. These vices can also be viewed as hurdles that runners in a race have to overcome.

The Fitness-Training Program

Columbanus's program consisted of the following elements:

1. To acquire mastery over personal drives by doing without good, as well as bad, things.

2. To develop positive strengths by doing good works. The purpose of this was to learn to channel energy creatively that had previously been used negatively.

3. To instill a habit of appreciation, particularly of God's presence in all things and at all times. The chanting of psalms was the main method.

4. To start a healing process by making restitution to any wronged person.

The program was voluntary, though in the case of monks and nuns it was part of the contract they made at the outset of their monastic lives. The Soul Friend would find out from the Seeker his weak points. These would be shared in complete trust, in an outpouring of the soul, known as confession.

Let's take a look at how the early Celtic training programs, particularly those of Columbanus, dealt with the eight hurdles to spiritual integrity.

GLUTTONY

Although we think of gluttony as exclusively excessive eating, it could also be excessive drinking, sleeping, or talking—in fact, any otherwise healthy activity that is carried to an extreme. Doing without is the principal remedy, but in a way that helps to overcome the vice. Columbanus inducted over-sleepers to prayer vigils during night hours, excessive talkers to extra periods of silence.

Seekers today may fall prey to excessive TV-watching, Internet-surfing, or shopping. A Soul Friend should have creative alternatives to suggest.

AVARICE

This is the love of money, which can lead to stealing, cheating, lying, manipulative business practices, or workaholism that robs family and friends of our presence. Columbanus's antidote was to foster generosity in the Seeker, which develops both others' trust and the Seeker's trust in God's providence. One exercise was for a Seeker to give money to the poor. A Seeker who had stolen from somebody was to repay the individual, not from savings, but from the earnings of her own work, in weekly installments. That kind of exercise has the added benefit of helping the Seeker put herself in the shoes of the other person; it inculcates service as the model of supreme achievement.

Anger is an acid
that can do more harm
to the vessel in which it
is stored than to anything
on which it is poured.

—MARK TWAIN

RAGE

Rage can find expression as verbal abuse, violence to a person or property, and murder. The inclusion of these acts under the heading of rage is perceptive. It shows that Columbanus's training program addressed the roots as well as the symptoms.

The remedies were varied, but they all aimed to bring about a deep change of heart. The tendency to quarrel had to be replaced with understanding, damage to property with replacement items, injury with medical attention, angry words with acts of forgiveness, and murder with an offer of time and effort in lieu of that which the dead person might have given. The Seeker who had no money had to work for the wronged person.

In our society, the element of personal restitution has been lost. Young people who vandalize do not have to make personal restoration because they do not earn income, and it is not administratively cost-effective (in the short term) to oversee this. Insurance companies cover car drivers who cause damage through road rage. A popular movement toward voluntary restitution could have a leavening effect.

But what can be achieved in the context of Soul Friendship far outweighs that which can be accomplished by any public program. Columbanus sought to replace rage with its opposite—love. Tears that flowed as the Seeker poured out her heart to her Soul Friend led to a deep receiving of forgiveness and a love for the person who had been wronged.

SELF-PITY

Small-mindedness, resentment, miserableness, indifference, and self-induced despair are all facets of self-pity. This despair is to be distinguished from what later was termed "the dark night of the soul," which was not a sinful attitude but rather a sacred desert experience.

The primary cure for self-pity was joy. Columbanus urged all young people to expect trials and disappointments from the outset, but to look upon these as opportunities for growing more selfless, and therefore more receptive to the unending joy that is God's gift and their destiny. A chief means of moving into joy is by chanting psalms, which are full of praise.

We cannot cure
the world of sorrows,
but we can choose
to live in joy.

—JOSEPH CAMPBELL[3]

LUST

The Penitentials provide training programs of varying intensity for adultery, fornication, child abuse, sex with animals, and self-abuse. In order to gain mastery over craving, fasting from food as well as from sex (even within marriage) was prescribed. The Seeker undertook not to live again in the same house with a person who had been a sexual partner, unless they got married. If a man had violated a virgin, he would pay compensation. A person who had abused a child would undertake one year's fast, a reduced intake of foods.

How can restitution be made by a married man who has a baby by another man's wife? This common failing devastates both the innocent wife and the innocent husband: their deepest bond of trust has been violated. Respect, trust, innocence, and love—all have been severely damaged. How can a healing process get underway that is not just a plastering over of the wound? How can a guilty man prove to both victims and to his collaborating sex partner who shares his guilt, that a professed change of heart is real? Columbanus's drastic remedy was for him to be celibate for three years, even with his wife. The desire that had threatened to destroy him had to be mastered.

*Therefore we
ought to live
as having to give
account to God*

> of our way of life
> every day.

—SAYINGS OF THE DESERT FATHERS[4]

Columbanus was wise to admit his partial knowledge. In the light of modern research into sexual therapeutic processes, it may be sensible to bring the wronged wife into the decision-making. She might welcome a period of abstinence to help her overcome her own revulsion at the unfaithful act, but sooner or later she may again desire and need sexual intercourse with her husband. Columbanus's principle can be retained if sexual intercourse is not resumed until it has been prepared for with prayer.

In our confused society, sexual experimentation is often thought to be a good thing. The Celtic guides knew that multiple sexual relationships tend to become depersonalized. These relationships may lack integrity, since real depth cries out for faithfulness, shared sacrifice, and single-mindedness before and after the event. They understood that this applied to both homosexuality and heterosexuality. Much modern insight confirms the wisdom of this.

The sex drive is one of the most powerful forces in life, for good or ill, and the purpose of the Celtic penitential programs was to bring order to it. The natural energies that the love drive represents should not be pushed down, but they should be harnessed so that they support and enhance life rather than bring destruction to self or others. In Celtic spirituality, sex is a good servant but a bad master. This means the sex drive must never be split off from the Spirit. Detached sexuality, which is not part of a deepening relationship with another and with God, is exploitive and can damage both partners emotionally.

What if the Seeker frequently fails in sexual morality? Discernment is necessary, to know whether the Seeker fundamentally wants to choose God or not. Rather than propose unrealistic goals, which lead to guilt, fear of the Soul Friend, and a downward spiral, it may be better to aim to first gradually reduce the number of lapses.

SLACKNESS

This includes neglect of duties, oversleeping, unreliability, wandering off without notice, lack of attentiveness to others, carelessness, and slipshod work. Training exercises include doing extra work on behalf of someone else, keeping prayer vigils during normal hours of sleep, and chanting psalms when sleepy.

During Columbanus's day, sleep was thought of as an image of death, and wakeful activity was an imitation of the Creator. The aim was to motivate the Seeker to a life of zeal, stability, perseverance, and excellence, and in this way to become an icon of God.

*The soul's joy
lies in doing.*

—PERCY BYSSHE SHELLEY

"What is your secret?" I asked my friend Derek, who had been a major in the British army, a shop steward in a laundry, and a tireless church worker into his eighties.

"The battle for the day is won or lost at the moment of waking," he told me. "If you let the downward pull of the flesh dominate you at the start of the day, and fail to get up the moment you wake up, everything else in your life will be lethargic."

VANITY

Vanity can be expressed as boasting, self-promotion, or causing discord through the promotion of ideas that are not God-centered (heresy). The Celtic fitness program required a Seeker to be accountable to another person, and to embrace self-imposed silences during meetings. A Seeker who had fostered discord through sectarian or heretical ideas had to publicly condemn these, and also to work to win back to unity in the faith those whom the Seeker's influence had led astray.

Columbanus geared his programs to the concept of life as a pilgrimage. The aim was to produce Christ-followers with trusting, childlike attitudes, who never thought that they knew it all. A Soul Friend whose Seeker has everything buttoned up should encourage the Seeker to attend to how others perceive him, and should point him to desert-style experiences where he can get in touch with his vulnerabilities.

PRIDE

A disregard of those in authority, envy, complaining, criticism, and contempt of others are all aspects of pride. Acts of humility are prescribed for those who struggle with pride. The training exercise to overcome envy is to practice kindness toward those the Seeker most envies. Defamation of another is seen as a sin against justice and love, so the culprit has to openly admit and apologize for this. The role of the Soul Friend is to affirm what is good in the accused person; to confront, correct, and elicit compassion in the Seeker. Columbanus's aim was always to excite a passion to be like Christ. So his training program includes taking to heart Christ's example of humility.

In your relationships
with one another,
have the same mindset
as Christ Jesus: Who,
being in very nature God,
did not consider equality
with God something
to be used to his own
advantage; rather, he
made himself nothing
by taking the very nature
of a servant, being made
in human likeness.
And being found in
appearance as a man,
he humbled himself
by becoming obedient to death—
even death on a cross!

—PHILIPPIANS 2:5–8 NIV

Behind all these penitential practices lay the concept of accountability. Soul friendships were sustained from that perspective. Mrs. Concannon, reflecting upon mutual influences in the lives of Columbanus and Francis of Assisi (who made devotion to Columbanus as his foundation at Bobbio), writes of the former: "His mission of penance was accomplished in that ministry of 'Soul Friendship' which did so much to build the laity into the solid masonry of the Church."[5]

The Relevance of Penance Today

Sportspeople often say that confidence comes as a result of training to the utmost. Spiritual training has much the same effect. Those who enrolled in the fitness-training programs described in this chapter were motivated by the love of God to give their utmost, and many of these ordinary people grew confident in God. In later generations, guilt and traditional expectation played a part in maintaining these training programs, and their innocence and integrity became tarnished.[6] Just as sports training has updated its tools and facilities, so has the training of athletes of the spirit.

A Soul Friend today might wish to introduce the idea of fitness training and ascertain whether the Seeker wishes to include this as part of the contract between them. No one today would wish to copy the precise regimen used by Columbanus. The principles, however, have never been bettered, and are, I believe, due for a come-back, as is indicated in this twenty-first-century psychology article on the seven deadly sins:

> The original deadly sins were inspired by humankind's perpetual struggle to rise above animalistic instincts and rein in the emotions. . . . To postpone gratification today for tomorrow's greater reward. To sacrifice our own needs for the good of others. It's our frequent inability to achieve this level of control that makes the sins as relevant today as they ever were. . . . "In my view self-control is the 'master virtue' underlying almost all others," says Roy Baumeister at Florida State University, an expert on self-control and the author of *Your Own Worst Enemy: Understanding the Paradox of Self-Defeating Behavior*. "Each of the deadly sins can be seen as a failure or breakdown of self-control." Baumeister's research has shown that self-restraint is like a muscle—the more you use it, the stronger it gets.[7]

Faithful are the
wounds of a friend

—PROVERBS 27:6 KJV

How May a Soul Friend Apply Penance Today?

If a Seeker is facing external problems caused by internal failures and asks a Soul Friend's help, the Soul Friend should focus on two things: the best way the Seeker can make restitution, and the best meditation exercise for building up self-mastery. Here is one example:

Brian was a zealous Christ-follower in his twenties. After being repeatedly betrayed by his fiancée, his anger erupted, he felt God had let him down, and he turned his back on God and decided to live for himself. He took a holiday flight overseas and made a girl pregnant. She decided to keep the baby, but she and Brian had nothing in common. Back home, Brian was riddled with guilt and eventually sought out a Soul Friend whom he had known from his past. How did the Soul Friend respond?

First, the Soul Friend asked Brian to tell the whole story. The Seeker needs to "get everything out," and the Soul Friend needs the full picture. Second, they decided what they needed to do during this time. There were four phases, each interspersed with plenty of space for Brian to be alone:

1. Talking through the anger and getting to its roots: Brian confessing it in prayer, the Soul Friend praying for release and healing.

2. Talking through the guilt, identifying steps of restitution (payments to the mother of 15 percent of Brian's salary until the baby was eighteen years old, monthly contact by phone; the offer of a month together with the child each year; the offer to bring up the child if the mother ever relinquished her); identifying the unmet emotional needs (lack of parental love) that had led Brian to try and meet these needs inappropriately; adopting a repetitive spiritual exercise that would develop mastery of these spiritual needs (an exercise meditating on the Mother-love of God was chosen that Brian agreed to repeat often); confession by Brian of sin and guilt, and prayer by the Soul Friend assuring him of God's forgiveness, encircling and releasing the baby and mother to God.

3. Preparing for the future, identifying the temperament and aptitudes of Brian, and envisioning a spiritual pattern he could follow

that would reflect these; affirming the need to abandon previous spiritual patterns that were driven by false church conditioning and were alien to Brian's nature; exploring contacts and books; and praying meditatively together

*If we confess our sins,
God is faithful and just
and will forgive our sins
and purify us from
all unrighteousness.*

—1 JOHN 1:9 NIV

Confession and Soul Friendship

Many Christ-followers who do not believe they need to confess their sins to a priest or to receive formal absolution, nevertheless confess sins to a nonordained Soul Friend, believing that it is God who forgives. Preparation for confession may include silence, readings from Scripture, or prophetic prayer. Although, in general, Soul Friends should adhere to the link between confession and restitution, we should not be legalistic about this. Confession might be followed by anointing with oil if this helps a Seeker go forth healed and calmed.

Summary

Soul Friends in Celtic monasteries used Penitentials produced by their monastic leaders as a tool to build up Seekers. These Penitentials were based on two principles: the need to make restitution for sins against other people, and the need to develop self-mastery. A contemporary Soul Friend should also have tools with which to develop restitution and self-mastery.

EXERCISES

For Soul Friends or potential Soul Friends.

1. Carefully go through each of the eight vices listed in this chapter. Think of an example of each vice that has damaged the experience of yourself or someone you know. Now prayerfully think through a training exercise and suggest a remedy that would help to master each of these sins.

2. Make a list of other vices that you think should be added to this list, and write out a training exercise for each.

3. In my example, "Brian" made a sixty-hour visit to a Soul Friend. If you were the Soul Friend, how might you use those sixty hours?

4. Use your imagination to reconstruct another example. Decide how you as the Soul Friend would use the time together, and what restitution and self-mastery exercises you would recommend.

Further Reading

Celebration of Discipline by Richard Forster (HarperOne, 2018). This book contains exercises that help develop self-mastery.

Notes

1. *Sancti Columbani Opera*, translated by G.S.M Walker (Dublin, EI: The Dublin Institute for Advanced Studies, 1970), contains the complete writings of Columbanus in English.

2. Oliver Davies. *Celtic Christianity in Early Medieval Wales: The Origins of the Welsh Spiritual Tradition* (Cardiff, UK: University of Wales Press), p. 85.

3. Joseph Campbell. *The Joseph Campbell Companion: Reflections on the Art of Living* (New York, NY: HarperCollins, 1991), p. 20.

4. Benedicta Ward, trans. *The Wisdom of the Desert Fathers: Systematic Sayings from the Anonymous Series of the Apophthegmata Patrum* (Oxford, UK: S.L.G. Press, 1986), p. 2.

5. Quoted in Anselmo M. Tommasini's *Irish Saints in Italy* (London, UK: Sands and Company, 1937).

6. For information on the Celtic Soul Friend's influence on the evolution of the sacrament of penance in the West, see O.D. Watkins' *A History of Penance* (London, UK: Longmans Green, 1920), vol. 2 on the Keltic System, and also James Dallen's *The Reconciling Community: The Rite of Penance* (New York, NY: Pueblo, 1986).

7. Christian Jarrett. "The Deadly Sins," *The Psychologist,* vol. 24, February 2011, pp. 89–104.

10
Order

Later Irish Monastic Insights into Soul Friendship

(the seventh to tenth centuries after Christ)

hen most of the Irish population became Christian, many monasteries became responsible for providing Soul Friends for the population through clergy, who developed this role in a ritualistic way. Lessons from these widespread practices were learned and were included in regulations that most monasteries put in place. Although

this was in many ways a retrograde development, the regulations contain warnings and advice from which we can learn.

A shift had taken place since the time of Brigid and Columba, several centuries earlier. Hermits and other wise individuals still acted as Soul Friends here and there, but in general, Soul Friendship became more ritualized and related to clergy, and therefore more male. People from the surrounding area flocked to their local monastery to confess and receive penances, and the monastery appointed one or more priests to make this their full-time ministry.

According to some historians of religious movements, it is an unwritten law that communities need reform at least every two centuries. The first generation or two remain fired up by the vision of their founder. Then, as success increases the size, bureaucracy replaces spontaneity; as disagreements arise, code replaces relationship; and what began as a movement becomes a monument. Fires lit by religious communities over the centuries tend to burn low after a few generations. To counter this, more detailed rules are laid down to maintain discipline and to prevent abuses.

The Soul Friend should look for candour and integrity in the confessions of Penitents.

> Fast and pray on behalf of these;
> if you don't, you will pay for it
> because the results of their sins
> will become a burden upon you.
>
> —RULE OF ST. CARTHAGE

In the eighth century, a reform movement began in Ireland that was known as *Celi De*, meaning the Servants of God. The reform sought to wean members of communities from formalism and kindle in them prayer, sensitivity, and unity of heart with like-minded Christ-followers, while acknowledging that they needed to organize in order to provide ministry on a large scale.

Rules of monasteries that embraced these reforms in the eighth and ninth centuries have come down to us, some in fragmentary form.[1] They reveal the pivotal role of the Soul Friend, both for monks and for laypeople who looked to the monastery for nurture. A monastic Soul Friend was grounded in the Scriptures and in the Rules of the saints. Among the monks and nuns, daily confession was as normal and useful as sweeping the floor. Correction "without harshness, and without blame, and with laughter" was the aim, rather than reproof. In spiritual direction, two things were all important: counsel and mortification.

In this chapter, we shall record extracts from the various Rules drawn up by monasteries that accepted reforms in the eighth century. The Rules are often named after the founder of the community, although they were written some centuries after the founder's death. It may be that during the twenty-first century, the church will face a larger-scale demand for the provision of Soul Friends. If so, we shall find useful advice from these Celtic monasteries.

> The monastery should have
> a priest who is devout
> and faithful to the monastic life,
> steadfast in his ministry,
> and a sure and compassionate
> guide in the art of good living.
>
> —THE RULE OF AILBE

The Rule of Ciaran (Seventh or Eighth Century): "Wander Only to Consult Wise People"

A partial copy exists of a Rule attributed to Saint Ciaran. If this refers to the Ciaran who founded Clonmacnoise Monastery, this is no doubt because his monastery was later influenced by the Celi De reform. This fairly early Rule contains the following interesting advice: "It is dangerous to form the habit of leaving one's monastery unless it be to visit a church, to consult the wise, or to make the round of the cemeteries."

We learn from this that monks customarily traveled around in order to consult mentors or "the wise." These were monks who suddenly wandered off at the prompting of their hearts, which made life difficult for the rest of the community who had to keep the organization going—and so they were warned against doing this.

The Rule of Comghall (Late Eighth Century): "Place Yourself Under Another"

This Rule, attributed to Comghall, the founder of the famous monastery at Bangor, includes these strong words: "The advice of a devout sage is a great asset if one wishes to avoid penalty. However self-confident you are, place yourself under the direction of another."

The Rule of Tallaght (Eighth Century)

The village of Tallaght, near Dublin, was built on the site of the monastery founded by Mael-Ruain, who died in 792, and who was a leader of the reform movement. *The Annuls of Ulster* mentions Mael Dithruib, a hermit who was a great friend and disciple of Mael-Ruain, and who kept a record of his sayings. These give us insights into their approach to Soul Friendship. The summaries that follow are from this record.

PREPARATION FOR A SOUL-FRIEND SESSION

Those of the laity who came for spiritual direction were ordered to remain apart from their wives on the nights of Wednesday, Thursday, and Saturday. When they did likewise on Sundays and during their wives' monthly periods, it was in line with the teaching of Peter, at least according to the Vatican's *Liber Clementinis*.

THE BASIS OF SOUL FRIENDSHIP

A person enters God's service when she promises what she has set out to do and takes this upon herself under the direction of someone else.

THE PERILS OF A SOUL FRIEND

Mael Dithruib used to say that the office of Soul Friend was perilous because, should the Soul Friend impose on a penitent a penance commensurate with the gravity of the sin, it was more likely to be breached than observed. But if the Soul Friend did not impose a penance, the debts of the sinner would fall upon himself. "There are those," he said, "who regard counsel as penance enough." It is safer for the Soul Friend to send them advice but not to receive their confession.

WHEN TO STOP BEING A SOUL FRIEND

Elair rejected all those whom he had accepted previously for spiritual direction because they would not give their best effort, and because they concealed some of their sins in confession. He would allow no one to approach him for the purpose of spiritual direction. He did, however, allow and encourage penitents, for their peace of soul, to go and question devout men, that is monks of perfect life who would have some proficiency in teaching what would be beneficial for their souls. He himself, however, did not receive anyone for spiritual direction, anyone, that is, whom he suspected had a director of his own from whom he might receive counsel.

CHANGING A SOUL FRIEND

Mael-Ruain was of like mind. He was unwilling to accept even Mael-Dithruib until he learned whether Mael-Dithruib already had a spiritual father to direct him. When Mael-Dithruib first came to Mael-Ruain for spiritual direction, Mael-Ruain said that "artisans such as smiths and carpenters do not like to see those whom they are training go to another craftsman for instruction. Why then should your spiritual father be happy to see you come to me for direction?"

"It is for that very reason," replied Mael-Dithruib, "that I obtained from my spiritual father permission to come to you." Mael-Ruain then agreed to become his director, and Mael-Dithruib submitted himself to his authority.

WHAT KIND OF SOUL FRIEND TO PLACE YOURSELF UNDER

Mael-Ruain then said to Mael-Dithruib: "We regard the first year spent under our spiritual direction as a year of purifying, and so you will have to spend three periods of forty days on bread and water, except for a mouthful of milk and water." And he added: "When you place yourself under the guidance and control of someone else, you should seek out the fire which will most fiercely burn, that is, which will spare you the least." This throws light upon the seriousness with which spiritual guidance was taken. The principle is one we can adopt to our benefit.

> Instruct the unlearned,
> both by what you teach
> and by the life that you model,
> so that they follow your example
> rather than sin.
>
> —RULE OF ST. CARTHAGE

The Rule of Saint Carthage (Ninth Century): Integrity

A Rule has come down to us from the ninth century, which has sometimes been attributed to Saint Carthage, who was abbot of a large monastery near Offaly in the eighth century. Copies of this Rule are in the British Museum and in Trinity College, Dublin. The Rule includes an entire section on the duties of the clerical Soul Friend. Reading between the lines, we can see that a large section of the population must have come to one or more priests set aside by their monastery for the full-time work of spiritual direction. Soul Friendship had almost become an industry, and with it came abuse. You can see also that when a priest was in great demand and lived off donations, he could easily find himself giving more time to some than to others.

Here is a paraphrase of some pieces of advice from the Rule:

> If you are a Soul Friend to someone, do not neglect him just because he has no money to offer you; and refuse to accept a donation from anyone who refuses to take seriously your advice. Take care not to let those who give you large donations have a hold on your affections; instead, let them be like fire on your body. Do not begrudge giving time and attention to those who can give you nothing, for the integrity of your soul is worth more than money. Indeed, you must share the spiritual treasures God has given you with everyone: strangers, even though they have no high connections; the poor; the elderly; the widowed—though not with people who are intent only on sin.

This raises the issue of charging for spiritual direction. Generally, in Britain and Ireland in recent centuries, no charges were made because most Soul Friends were already provided for by the church if they were a priest, pastor, or a member of a religious community. Increasingly, today, this is not so, and Seekers should be responsible in giving donations to Soul Friends who are not otherwise supported. However, there is a warning to such Soul Friends: never refuse spiritual direction to someone just because she cannot afford to pay. This marks out a difference between Christian ministry and commercial secular agencies.

Each person should be
treated the same
in simplicity and complete
confidentiality.

—RULE OF ST. CARTHAGE

INSTITUTIONALISM

Institutionalism, even superstition, crept into the church over the centuries. The Celi De, which began as a reform, acquiesced to abuses. A Rule of the Celi De from the eleventh or twelfth century reveals a bureaucrat's approach to Soul Friendship. The Rule states that there should be a bishop for every territory, though in the early years of Christianization, people-groups, not territories, had bishops. The bishop's duties included that of being a Soul Friend to rulers (presumably holy hermits or foster mothers were not considered fitting now). Each area had a parish priest who had students he prepared for ordination. Any priest who took upon himself the care of a church also took upon himself the duty of giving spiritual direction to all the "subjects" (sic) of that church, men, women, and children. Anyone who refused the guidance of this spiritual father was to be denied Communion or inclusion in the Intercessions. Was the power game, from which the Irish church had for centuries been so gloriously free, now entrenched at its heart?

The role of the Soul Friend soon became fully institutionalized throughout the pre-Reformation Western church. In 1215, the Fourth Lateran Council made confession to a priest obligatory. Although nuns no doubt continued to give spiritual direction within certain circles, Soul Friendship as a creative bond between two free spirits was a thing of the past.

After the Reformation, the Roman Catholic Church at the Council of Trent (sixteenth century) defined Confession as one of the Seven Sacraments of the Church. More recently, the Catholic Church has renamed this the Sacrament of Reconciliation, in an attempt to recover something of the human process involved in it.

The churches that broke away from Roman control during the fifteenth- and sixteenth-century Reformation rejected clericalism and compulsory confession; they believed in "the priesthood of all believers." This did not, however, lead to a revival of the role of the Soul Friend. Instead, almost all the practices of the old church were now suspect, and spiritual direction had been too closely identified with the priesthood to be allowed back in a lay form. In theory, members of Reformed churches were encouraged to "confess their sins to one another" as the New Testament letter of James urges (5:16), but this was not practical in village communities where gossip abounded.

The Church of England, which claimed to embrace the best of the old church and the Reformed churches, did, in time, restore spiritual direction as a valued part of its tradition. Although its formularies do not mention it, it has taught this about the making of confessions: "All may, none must, some should." It has taken a similar approach to spiritual direction in general. The spiritual director need not be, but often has been, a priest. Although the Church of England proclaims belief in the priesthood of all believers, spiritual direction tended in practice to be restricted to its more Catholic wing, and to bookish people who could afford to stay at retreat houses.

The wheel has now come full circle. The freedoms of travel and information that ushered in the third millennium have made possible, and indeed necessary, a new flowering of Soul Friendship that transcends, though it does not devalue, the Church's formal arrangements of the past. If there is a large-scale revival of Soul Friendship, some of the lessons of this chapter will need to be learned.

Summary

As enormous numbers of adults in Ireland joined the church and expected to have a Soul Friend, the provision of a Soul Friend was organized from the top down, and the spontaneity of early days was lost. This was the price of success. Eventually, the confession of sins to an allocated (male) priest replaced Soul Friendship as the norm in spiritual direction. This form went into steep decline at the close of the second millennium. Today's multichoice society, with the many possibilities that the Internet affords, makes possible a revival of the original type of Soul Friendship.

EXERCISES

For a Soul Friend

1. Consider how the Rule of Tallaght advised people to prepare for Soul Friendship sessions. How do you recommend yourself or others to prepare?

For a Soul Friend or Seeker

2. According to the Rule of Tallaght, people enter God's service when they promise to adhere to what they have set out to do under the direction of someone else. Are you and your Soul Friend clear what you have set out to do? If not, work on this now, and write it down to discuss with your Soul Friend when you next meet.

For a Seeker

3. Elair refused to be a Soul Friend to people who only told him half the truth. Do you have a Soul Friend (or, if not, a priest or pastor) to whom you can truthfully entrust your deepest faults and longings? If so, have you confided all? If not, what should you do about it?

Read More

The Celtic Monk: Rules and Writings of Early Irish Monks translated by Uinseann Ó Maidin (Cistercian Publications, 1996). You can find here several complete Rules from the Irish monastics.

Note

1. These Rules are printed in English in Uinseann O Maidin's *The Celtic Monk: Rules and Writings of Early Irish Monks* (Kalamazoo, MI: Cistercian Publications, 1996). I have adopted the scholarly consensus as to the dating of the Rules that this book records. Most of the Rules other than Tallaght's were written some two centuries after the death of the saint in whose name they were composed. In some cases, this attribution may have been simply a dedication to the founder of the monastery concerned.

11
An Art

Aelred's Insights into Soul Friendship

(the twelfth century after Christ)

Aelred had a great gift of friendship; he studied it, fostered it, and wrote about it. Although much of what he wrote is about friendship in a general sense, we, with him, can view that general friendship as the base of a pyramid. Near the top of the pyramid, certain friendships meet the criteria that mark a Soul Friend.

Aelred's great-grandfather looked after Saint Cuthbert's shrine at Durham, which was one of the few parts of Northumbria's Celtic heritage to survive the ravages of the Vikings. This devotion to Cuthbert was handed down through the married priests in his family, and was continued by Aelred's father, Eilaf. Eilaf had to leave his post at Cuthbert's shrine and retire to Hexham when William the Conqueror, at the pope's urging, began to enforce clerical celibacy. Here Aelred, who was named Ethelred in his early years, was born. Soon monks replaced married clergy there, too, so in 1118, Eilaf entered Durham's new cathedral monastery of Saint Cuthbert, in the presence of Ethelred and his two brothers. There, a call to the monastery began to stir in the young Ethelred.

A custom of that first feudal age was that sons of members of the upper class were sent away to be fostered by a person of high influence and education. Ethelred was sent over the border to the court of David, King of the Scots. There, he proved most popular and made close friends with David's two stepsons, Simon and Waldef, who became models for him. It was probably there, too, that his Anglo-Saxon name was softened to the Norman form by which he is now known.

Friendship is . . .
a bridge between us
and the perfect love of God.

—AELRED[1]

During his childhood education, Aelred became familiar with the dialogue of the Roman philosopher Cicero, *On Friendship*, which influenced him ever after. At the royal court, he had the opportunity to develop a variety of good friendships, for which he had a great aptitude. Yet he recorded that even friends whose company he most enjoyed did not enter into the things that went on deep inside him, and this sometimes brought him near to despair. His were highly successful social friendships, but they lacked the spiritual element.

In 1134, while returning from a visit to York on church business, Aelred called in at the new Cistercian monastery at Rievaulx. The impact on him was so powerful that he offered himself as a novice there and was accepted. He got on as well with everyone there as he had at the royal court, and before long, his abbot sent him to Rome to represent the monastery. On his return to Rievaulx, Aelred was appointed Master of Novices; then he was sent to found a new monastery at Revesby, and in 1147, he was recalled to become Abbot of Rievaulx. His duties included regular visits to a daughter monastery at Wardon.

Aelred brought a fresh approach to monastic life. The old attitude had been that monks should have no special friendships and should therefore not express affection. Aelred had no place for friendships that shut out anyone else or that did not respect boundaries, but he did not believe in suppressing pure, thoughtful friendships that grew out of the flow of personalities given to God. In this respect, the Celtic way of seeing the Presence of God in human lives triumphed over the formal, standardized approach that had by then become the norm in the church.

Aelred's work *Spiritual Friendship* reflects this new attitude that was restoring the spirit of friendship that marked Celtic Christians such as Saint Cuthbert. The work consists of three books, the first of which was probably begun at Wardon, while the third was completed some twenty years later. The framework owes much to Cicero's treatise *On Friendship*, with its questions and answers. Much of the content of Aelred's work, however, explores the transforming power of Christ as the source and sustainer of friendship that embraces the soul and is eternal.

We know that Aelred drew inspiration from the Celtic saints. When he wrote *The Life of St. Ninian*,[2] he lamented that in his own time, "mouths consecrated for the praise of God are daily polluted by backbiting" and contrasted this with Ninian, "the radiant one," "whose miracles do not cease to shine forth even to our own times." Aelred compared Ninian to a bee "who formed for himself the honeycombs of wisdom." There seems little doubt that Aelred sought to do likewise, and that this was reflected in his Soul Friendships.

The rest of this chapter are paraphrased extracts from Aelred's work.

> Here we are, you and I,
> and I hope that Christ
> makes a third with us.
> No one can interrupt us now. . . .
> So come now, dearest friend,
> reveal your heart
> and speak your mind.
>
> —AELRED

Book One:
Questions About General Friendship

When I was a boy I loved to give affection to my friends, but because I did not know the laws of friendship, I was pulled in all directions. Once I had read Cicero's treatise on friendship, I had something against which to check my changing affections. Then, when I committed my life to serve Christ in a monastery, Christ and his words in the Scriptures became the center of my affections. But I never forgot Cicero's thoughts about friendship, so I wrote my own treatise on spiritual friendship, drawing on the Scriptures and the friendships of Christian saints.

Ivo: I should like to learn how the friendship that ought to exist among us begins and is sustained in Christ, of whom Cicero was ignorant.

Aelred: You can get an imperfect idea of the nature of friendship in this definition of Cicero's: *It is mutual harmony in human and Divine affairs coupled with love and care.*

Ivo: How does true friendship relate to those who live with Christ?

Aelred: The word friend (in Latin *amicus*) comes from the word love (*amor*). I have explained the affections and movements of love in my book *Mirror of Charity*. A friend is a guardian of mutual love. He guards my spirit so as to preserve its secrets in faithful silence; he should endure the defects he finds in my spirit, rejoice and sorrow with me, and feel as his own all that his friend experiences. Friendship therefore consists of ties of love and sweetness. A true friend offers unconditional love at all times, whatever the other may do wrong.

Although friendship is so difficult to achieve, it is possible. Remember that Jesus said: "Ask, and you shall receive." The early Christians received this grace. We read in the Acts of the Apostles that they "were of one heart and mind" (4:32). How many martyrs gave their lives for their brothers and sisters? "No one has greater love than the one who lays down their life for their friends," Jesus said (John 15:13).

Ivo: Is there a difference between love and friendship?

Aelred: Yes, for God requires us to love our enemies as well as our friends. We only call those people friends to whom we can entrust our hearts and all their secrets.

Ivo: Don't godless people have such bonds, too?

Aelred: They may have a harmony of vices, but this cannot

be called spiritual friendship. For the person who loves sin hates himself, and will not be able to love another. The fact that even friendships polluted by lust, greed, or comfort are so valued only goes to show how much more precious is pure friendship.

Selfish friendship lusts after people as objects for gratification. Friendships that are inflamed by lust or greed are not open to reason, or to the judgment of others. That kind of friendship manipulates and becomes consumed by deceit. It carries within it the seeds of its own destruction.

In contrast true, spiritual friendship springs from the feelings of the heart, which have their own dignity, and no ulterior motive. This kind of friendship is born of those who share a similar calling in God. Prudence directs, justice rules, fortitude guards, and self-control moderates this kind of friendship.

Ivo: What is the source of friendship in the Divine plan?

Aelred: God built companionship into all creation; not one created thing exists alone. It is the same in the spiritual world and among the angels. Pleasant companionship and delightful love among the angels enabled them, though they have free will, never to have envy or discord. Finally, when God created human beings, God said it was not good for humans to be alone; that is why there are men and women. From the beginning, nature implanted the desire for friendship and love in the heart of each person.

However, after the fall into sin, human beings became divided by envy. Friendship was violated by the many and only lived by the few. Law was brought in to regulate friendship, and to put bounds upon the power of sin to destroy it. Although many so-called friendships have mixed motives, it is possible for people who do not serve God to get a taste of natural friendship through these, so that they then want to find true friendship and wisdom.

Ivo: What is the link between wisdom and friendship?

Aelred: Friendship is inextricably linked to wisdom. This may surprise you, but if true friendship is eternal, we see that wisdom consists in following what is true and everlasting. As the Scripture says: "The person who lives in God lives in friendship." In this sense, we can say that God is friendship.

No medicine is more valuable,
none more efficacious,
none better suited
to the cure of all our
temporal ills than a friend

to whom we may turn
for consolation in time
of trouble, and with whom
we may share our
happiness in time of joy.

—AELRED

Book Two:
The Blessings of Friendship

Walter: What are the practical advantages of friendship?

Aelred: Nothing more sacred is striven for, nothing more useful is sought after, nothing more difficult is discovered, nothing sweeter is experienced, and nothing more profitable is possessed. For friendship bears fruit in this life and the next.

It combats vices by its own virtue, it tempers adversity, moderates prosperity, and assuages loneliness. What happiness, security, and joy to have someone to whom you dare to speak on equal terms as to yourself; one to whom you need not fear to confess your failings; one to whom you can without embarrassment share your progress in the life of the Spirit; one to whom you can entrust the secrets of your heart and before whom you can place all your plans. Friendship heightens the joys of prosperity and lessens the sorrows of adversity by sharing them. It is the best medicine in life. More than all these, friendship is a bridge between us and the perfect love of God.

In friendship, there is no pretense; it is holy, voluntary, and true. Its adjuncts are honor and charm, truth and joy, sweetness and goodwill, affection and action. The ever-flowing inspiration of the love by which we love our friend is Christ.

A good goal of friendship is that we behave toward our friend as we would like our friend to behave toward ourselves. True friendship is therefore only possible among good people. For as long as one delights in something that is not good more than in the good of another, one cannot be truly that person's friend.

OBJECTIONS

Gratian: But surely I am not good, so how can I have such friendship?

Aelred: I mean by a good person someone who by God's grace, as Saint Paul writes, lives a self-controlled, godly, and upright life (Titus 2:12).

Walter: I wonder whether friendship is so difficult that it is best avoided. Are not my own burdens enough to bear, without having to bear those of a friend? Since it is so difficult to keep loving someone even to death, isn't it better not to start than to let someone down later?

Aelred: What is the wisdom of avoiding friendship in order to avoid care, burdens, or fears? Can you achieve moral growth in your own life without struggle? Then why expect to achieve mutual growth without struggle? Cicero reminds us that to take friendship out of life is like taking away the sun. Or take the example of Saint Paul, who was weak alongside the weak and strong alongside the strong. Do you think he should have given up those ways?

Walter: What sort of friendships should be avoided?

Aelred: As well as the so-called friendship that is based on interest in a common vice, the aimless friendship that pursues anyone who passes by without thought should be avoided. We should never follow physical attraction that lacks integrity, reason, and openness to others. We should guard against unfaithful, unstable, impure loves. This kind of relationship is better called friendship's poison than friendship. The beginnings of a spiritual friendship should possess purity of intention, direction of thought, and the restraint of a balanced spirit.

A friendship entered into for no other reason than to gain benefits is also unsound. Certainly, some benefits such as advice and understanding are lovely fruits of friendship, but they should not be the roots of it. The blessings proceed from the friendship; the friendship does not proceed from the blessings. As with biblical friendships such as that between David and Jonathan, it is not so much the benefits obtained through a friend that delights as the friend's love in itself.

The reward of
friendship is itself.
The one who hopes
for anything else
does not understand
what true friendship is.

—AELRED

Book Three: The Conditions, Limits, and Fruits of Friendship

Aelred: The source of friendship is love. Love can proceed from nature, as a mother loves her child; it can proceed from duty, such as the act of forgiving an enemy; or it can proceed from affection alone, as when a person's beauty, strength, personality, or character steals into the soul. Friendship should only proceed from the love that is both pure, according to reason, as well as affectionate, according to the heart. An impulse to affection that is not willing to be tested and weighed should be guarded against. We should never be ruled by only the head or by only the heart, but by both together. There can be love without friendship, but friendship without love is impossible.

The foundation of all true friendship is the love of God; all other attractions must be submitted to this. We cannot love another if we do not love ourselves, since we learn how to love our neighbor by doing to them what we wish for ourselves.

Not all whom we love should be embraced as friends. Since your friend is the companion of your soul, to whom you wish to entrust yourself completely, you should choose someone who is fitted for this. Then you should test this friendship and only then embrace it. For friendship should be stable and manifest a certain likeness to eternity. We should not, like children, change friends by whim. There is nothing more detestable than the person who injures, deserts, or insults a friend. A friend should be chosen with extreme care and tested with the utmost caution, for after that, the two should become as one.

The Four Stages of Soul Friendship

The four stages by which one attains such friendship are selection, probation, admission, and harmony.

SELECTION

We should draw our friends from that reservoir of people who seek to supplant anger with patience, and suspicion with the contemplation of love. These qualities undergird friendship: love—a delight in doing good to another; affection—an inward pleasure that is naturally expressed; security—the ability to keep intimacies so that there is no fear or suspicion; happiness—a friendly sharing of everything in our lives.

Avoid selecting as a friend someone with faults such as backbiting, impugning another's integrity, arrogance, breaking of a confidence, or secret undermining, which make this unattainable (Sirach 22:27). However, some persons may have faults, but they do not give way to the vices that break friendship; their faults can be confronted and healed, and they can then continue their friendship. Fickle, suspicious, talkative, or irritable persons can develop into good friends, but the healing process must be underway before you go further.

*Friendship is that virtue
by which spirits are
bound by ties
of love and sweetness
and out of many
are made one.*

—AELRED

PROBATION

These qualities must be tested in a friend: loyalty, right intention, discretion, and patience. Loyalty is friendship's nurse and guardian. With it, a friend remains a true companion through fortune and misfortune alike. A truly loyal friend sees nothing in her friend but her heart. By right intention, we mean that a friend should expect nothing from the friendship except God and the natural good that flows from this. By discretion, we mean an understanding of what to seek, do, and suffer for a friend; what to confront and what to affirm; and the manner, time, and place for these. Patience means that we do not hit back when our friend confronts something unacceptable in us, and that we faithfully bear adversity caused by something our friend does.

A friend of mine who lost his temper nevertheless did not break a confidence or impugn my integrity. Though he transgressed the law of friendship, that was no reason for me to cease to treat him with the utmost confidence and solicitude, since I have made that commitment.

Most of us fall into a fault at some time or another. When this happens to a friend, we should take great care to help him make amends and to put right what has gone wrong between us.

If your friend refuses to do this, if he breaks the foundations of friendship, or if he injures another person who is also your friend, then you are right to end the friendship. In this situation, we should make a gradual withdrawal of the friendship, little by little, so that it dies away without causing more harm. Even if a former friend hurls public abuse at us we should never wage war on someone who was once our friend. Even if friendship has to be withdrawn, love should still be shown, which will include traces of the former friendship.

ADMISSION

How can we cultivate friendship? By giving whenever our friend is in need, if possible before she needs to ask us. Do this in a way that preserves mutual cheerfulness and self-confidence. We should not, however, give promotions or honors on a basis of favoritism, and a true friend should never expect those sorts of rewards from the friendship. If we are in a position to appoint people to posts, we should not do this because they are friends, but because they are suited to the post. Think of Jesus, who appointed Peter to a chief post, but had such a profound rapport with John.

HARMONY

We can cultivate friendship by praying for and being solicitous of one another, and by taking pleasure in one another's progress. It can happen that as a person prays to Christ for a friend, the sweetness he finds in Christ passes over to that friend.

Give each other such respect that if your friend sins, you yourself blush and feel the pain of it. In this way, your very demeanor can help your friend to regain a right demeanor himself. Praise your friend often, but never be subservient. Offer advice and counsel from the heart, but not in a paternalistic or condescending way. If you perceive a fault developing in your friend, bring it to his attention in private, thus maintaining sympathy and respect. However, if he continues to resist, do it openly, even if it wounds him, but always without bitterness. The friend needs to feel that your correction is born of love, not rancor, so do not hide your feelings. It is good if your tears flow.

Study, too, your friend's type of personality, and adapt your responses to this. If she is under pressure, wait for an appropriate moment to sort out something that is wrong. To bide your time, not giving the impression that anything is wrong, is not the same as dissimulation, which is always wrong.

In true friendship there is equality of regard, regardless of the different social standing two friends may have. There is a preference of the other before self, as Jonathan, a king's son, preferred David before himself (1 Samuel 23:17). The best companion of friendship is reverence. True and eternal affection is where there is no deceit. It begins in this life and is completed in the next.

A PERSONAL EXAMPLE OF SOUL FRIENDSHIP

I will give you an example of friendship from my personal experience. I recall choosing one friend, when I was young, because we had similar interests. I demanded nothing and bestowed nothing but affection. He had no share in the burdens of my duties and died while still young. Another person was a co-worker who shared many burdensome duties with me; I only admitted him into the intimacy of friendship in later years. I was drawn to the first person through affection but was never able to test this. I was drawn to the second person through duty; he was tested over many years, and only then, as my admiration for his qualities grew, was affection born, and we became the closest confidantes. There was no pretense, evasion, or half-truths, but everything was open and above board. We corrected each other without getting indignant. He exposed himself to dangers and forestalled scandals on my account. He was the refuge of my spirit, the solace of my griefs, whose heart of love received me when I was worn out, whose counsel refreshed me when I was despondent. He calmed me when I was distressed and soothed me when I was angry. When anything unpleasant occurred I shared it with him so that we carried it together shoulder to shoulder. Was not this a foretaste of the blessedness of heaven? If you see anything in this example which is worth imitating, please make sure you profit from it.

There is more. Once as I walked amid my brothers in the monastery, the affection of all passed into my soul, and I was transfused by joy. As we ascend from the holy love with which we embrace a friend to the love with which we embrace Christ, fear, even of death, departs, and we partake of the spiritual fruit of friendship, wanting the fullness of heaven, when the friendship we have known on earth with a few shall be outpoured by God upon all, and all shall outpour upon God, and God shall be all in all.

Summary

Aelred restored the freshness, integrity, and spontaneity of friendship that had been overlaid with formality since the first flowering of the Celtic church. If we apply the principles of friendship that he expounds, we create the seedbed in which Soul Friendships can come to flower. Only one or two of the friendships Aelred describes can be described as true Soul Friendships. He, however, was limited to those who were members of his monastery; we are not.

EXERCISES
For all readers

1. Draw up a list of people you are acquainted with to whom you are naturally drawn. Cross out those with whom you could not sustain thoughtful, rounded conversations about things of the mind. Now cross out those with whom you could not sustain a sharing of the deep things of the spirit, because intimacies would either not be understood or not respected. If anyone remains on this list, what prevents you from taking further steps to develop the friendship?

2. Review in your life, in the light of what Aelred writes, these four qualities of a friend that need to be tested: loyalty through good and bad times; absence of "demand"; understanding of the developmental process in a relationship; willingness to be corrected.

3. Review your friendships in the light of these suggested ways of cultivating a friendship: mutual meeting of needs, prayer, high regard, encouragement, counsel, loving correction, transparency.

4. Contemplate heaven as the place of accelerated and maximum friendship.

Read More

Spiritual Friendship by Aelred of Rievaulx, translated by Mary Eugenia Laker (Ave Maria Press, 2008). This edition of the spiritual masterpiece is complemented by helpful commentary and reflection questions for each chapter.

Notes

1. Quotes throughout this chapter are taken from Aelred of Rievaulx's *Spiritual Friendship,* translated by Mary Eugenia Laker (Notre Dame, IN: Ave Maria Press, 2008).

2. *The Life of St. Ninian* by Aelred is included in *Two Celtic Saints: The Lives of Ninian and Kentigern* (Burnham-on-Sea, UK: Llanerch, 1989).

12
Dying

Soul Friends at Heaven's Door

(the sixth, seventh, and nineteenth centuries after Christ)

Soul Friendship that deepens into old age can be a deep solace when a person is dying. Stories from early Ireland and from nineteenth-century Scotland give us a feel for what a Soul Friend can offer at death. But there are limits to this. That is why we do well to learn how Celtic Christians made Soul Friends of those who were already in heaven.

When death draws near, we have no energy with which to keep up appearances. We need to be with those in whose presence we do not have to strive. We need someone who will hold our hand and be a bridge for us between earth and heaven. Soul Friends are there for each other at life-and-death moments.

The Celtic tradition places much value upon Soul Friends being present to one another at death. When Columba intuited that the monk Cailton would not live long, he sent a message inviting him to come to Iona to rest, "for, loving you as a friend, I want you to end your days with me here."

When Ciaran of Clonmacnoise was dying, he waited alone in his little chapel for his Soul Friend Kevin of Glendalough to arrive. Unfortunately, Ciaran died before Kevin arrived. However, we are told in *The Life of Ciaran,* that "Ciaran's spirit returned from heaven and reentered his body so that he could commune with Kevin and welcome him. The two friends stayed together from the one watch to another, engaged in mutual conversation, and strengthened their friendship. Then Ciaran blessed Kevin, and Kevin blessed water and administered the Eucharist to Ciaran. Ciaran gave his bell to Kevin as a sign of their lasting unity."[1]

When the Soul Friend of the aging Findbarr, whom we read about in chapter 7, died, Findbarr decided to ask an old priest named Oeling, of Aghabullogge, to become his new Soul Friend. God revealed to Oeling that Findbarr was to come, so Findbarr was received with great love by the whole of Oeling's household. During the remaining years of Oeling's life, they remained on the most intimate terms of friendship and confidence, but the grief of Findbarr at the death of a precious Soul Friend was again renewed when Oeling became terminally ill. Just before he died, he said to Findbarr, "I place you under the charge and guidance of Jesus Christ himself." Tradition says that then Jesus appeared and took the hand of Findbarr, and ever afterward he wore a glove on his hand to cover its resplendent brightness.

Sleep, sleep and away
with your sorrow
the great sleep of Jesus,
the restoring sleep of Jesus,
the sleep of the kiss
of Jesus of peace and glory,
on the arm of the Jesus of blessings. . . .
May kindly Michael,
Chief of the holy angels,
take charge of your beloved soul,
and tenderly bring it home
to the Three of limitless love,

> Creator, Saviour,
> Eternal Life-Giver.
>
> —*CARMINA GADELICA*

When Findbarr himself became ill, he visited his friend Colman at Cloyne; Findbarr became sicker and prepared for his death while on this visit. Colman sat beside his bed to the end. On September 25, 623, Findbarr yielded his soul to his Creator. His body was taken to Cork, where there was a twelve-day wake. One of those at the wake, Bishop Fursey of Ferns, saw a golden ladder reaching from the tomb to heaven.

To be fully present when we come to that time of final parting, we need to have embraced death as a friend. Our modern-day world goes to great lengths to deny the presence of death, but not so the Celts. It is said that Columba took back to Iona a clod of earth from the grave of his friend, Ciaran of Clonmacnoise, and that he took this with him wherever he went. The Rule of Columba urged all members to prepare for their deaths. Columba, Cuthbert, Brendan, and others received prophecies about the time and manner of their deaths; they died triumphantly.

A Soul Friend should prepare a Seeker for death. That means learning to transfigure the faces of death that leer at us on our journey through life. One face is fear. Fear is rooted in the fear of death, of loss, of the unknown. Death, for a Seeker who has been enabled to overcome fear, will be a meeting with a friend.

Fear flees as we become familiar with the company of heaven, and with the borderlands that form a bridge between earth and heaven. The company of Celtic Christians on earth became friends with the company of heaven. They also sensed that the saints of God in heaven have a role in our spiritual formation on earth. In the Celtic tradition, the world of heaven was seen to be so close to the world of earth that death was thought of as an opportunity more than a threat.

May God open
to me every pass.
Christ open to me
every narrow way.
Each soul of holy man
and woman in heaven
be preparing for me
my pathway.

—CARMINA GADELICA

A Soul Friend's Prayers at a Deathbed

In the folk memory of the nineteenth-century Hebrideans, "the Death-croon was chanted over the dying by the anamchara, the Soul Friend, assisted by three chanters."[2] Later on, the rite passed into the hands of the town elders and the mourning women, who eventually sold their services as a profession.

Alexander Carmichael tells us in his collection of Scottish prayers and traditions, the *Carmina Gadelica*, that prayers said by a Soul Friend over a dying person are known as a death blessing, a soul leading, or a soul peace. The Soul Friend makes the sign of the cross on the person's forehead and asks the Three Persons of the Trinity and the saints in heaven to receive the departing soul.

When the soul separates
from the body
and goes in bursts of light
up from out its human frame,
O holy God of eternity,
come to seek and find you.
May God and Jesus aid you.

> May God and Jesus protect you.
> May God and Jesus
> and the gentle Spirit
> eternally seek and find you.
>
> —*CARMINA GADELICA*

A member of staff at St. Christopher's Hospice for the dying in London told me that three things stand out as most important to a dying person: *relationship, rhythm*, and *creation*. A Soul Friend (even if it is a staff member who "stands in" as a Soul Friend in a patient's last weeks) can encourage the dying person to talk about his nearest and dearest, what he wants to say to them, when, and how. Letters and messages might be conveyed through the Soul Friend to dear ones who cannot be present. The Soul Friend may draw out whether the dying person has relatives or friends who need to be forgiven. Perhaps the dying person can voice his hurt or forgiveness to the Soul Friend. Ordinary rhythms—waking and sleeping, light and dark of the day and of the seasons—also give meaning to this time. The ongoingness of this life's rhythms reflects something of the other side, and provides reassurance and hope. Creation—the world of Nature—also deepens the death experience. A simple thing such as a ray of sun falling on a cheek becomes a cherished moment.

It is good for a Soul Friend to unfold memories for the one who is dying, to recall important events, to give assurance that there is nothing to fear. A dying person returns to the specialness of the moment, like a young child, so it matters that we too become present to the one who is dying—and become present to our own grief only when away from the bedside.

By the side of a dying loved friend, we feel helpless. But that very helplessness can be our best gift to the helpless friend. We can stay with her in peace, saying, "I am here," or stroking her in wordless prayer. From time to time, out of this silence, beautiful words of prayer may be spoken.

A Soul Friend may place a crucifix before the eyes of the frail or dying person. A well-known Bible passage, psalm, or hymn may be read, and further prayers may be repeated from time to time.

A PRAYER AT DEATH

In the Name of
the all-powerful Father,
in the Name of
the all-loving Son,
in the Name of

the enfolding Spirit,
I command all spirit
of fear to leave you.
I break the power
of unforgiven sin in you.
I set you free from
dependence upon human ties
that you may be as free as the wind,
as soft as sheep's wool,
as straight as an arrow;
and that you may journey
into the heart of God.

Angels as Soul Friends

I am told that in Gaelic the "you" in the blessing "God be with you" is in the plural; the meaning is: "God be with you and with your guardian angel."

Many of the Lives of Celtic saints refer to them developing a friendship with an angel. Adamnan's *Life of St. Columba* contains breathtaking accounts of his encounters with angels. David of Wales received significant guidance from his angel companion.

And before them, was Patrick. He may have had no

seniors to turn to in some of the areas where he labored, but one thing he had—his guardian angel. Some years after Patrick escaped slavery in Ireland, he had a dream in which a figure named Victor brought letters from the Irish, urging him to "come back and walk with us once more." Patrick himself records this. Writers some centuries later wrote about a guardian angel who guided Patrick throughout his life, and this guardian angel became identified with the dream figure Victor. According to the later writings, an angel used to visit Patrick every seventh day and talked to Patrick as one person talks to another. Even during his six years as a slave, the angel is said to have talked with him some thirty times.

When Patrick knew he would die soon, he made his way to his headquarters at Armagh. But an angel came to him during his journey there and said, "Why do you go on a journey without Victor's guidance? Victor calls you. Change your route and go to him." And Patrick did.

At the last, when we die,
we have the dear angels
for our escort on the way.
They who can grasp
the whole world in their hands
can surely also guard our souls

that they make
that last journey safely.

—MARTIN LUTHER

Heaven's Saints Pray for Us

MAKE FRIENDS OF THE DEAD

Jesus asked us to remember, when we think about our forbearers in the faith, that God is God of the living, not of the dead (Matthew 22:32). The Bible teaches us that through the birth, death, and resurrection of Jesus Christ, death has been vanquished; it no longer becomes a barrier between us and eternity. The belief of the church in Celtic days, concerning Christians who had died, was that they had joined an innumerable company of living witnesses to Christ (Hebrews 12: 22,23).

There is a strand in church teaching—based on 1 Thessalonians 4:13–18, where Paul refers to those who "sleep in Jesus"—that the soul is unconscious after death until it is awakened at Christ's Second Coming. This teaching did not appear until the fifteenth century, and it was alien to Celtic Christians. They understood death's "sleep" to be a deep peace rather than unconsciousness, a cessation of earthly activity but not of spiritual presence. We find many indications in Scripture that those who have died are alert and aware of what is taking place both in heaven and on earth. The Bible would not have called them "witnesses" if they were unconscious of their surroundings.

Christians believe that Christ is the Mediator between God and humans. We can, and do, pray directly to God through Christ. But that does not mean that we do not need human friends who pray for us. The Scriptures frequently command us to pray for one another (for example, 1 Timothy 2:1; Colossians 4: 2–4). The saints in heaven can answer our prayers no more and no less than can our friends on earth. They have no power to answer them of their own accord; they can only plead with Christ on our behalf—but since the departed remain alive in Christ, why should they cease to express their love and concern for us in prayer? Freed from the concerns of day-to-day survival on earth, more intimately knit to Christ than we are, they can intercede for us more frequently and powerfully than many an earth-bound friend.

The life and passion of a person leaves an imprint on the ether of a place.

> Love does not remain
> within the heart,
> it flows out to build
> secret tabernacles
> in a landscape.
>
> —JOHN O'DONOHUE[3]

MONENNA

When the local people of Killeevy, in sixth-century Ireland, learned that their much-loved founding abbess Monenna was on her deathbed, they asked her, as those who were linked to her by blood and by the spirit, to give them one more year of her presence with them, for they knew that God would give her whatever she asked. She replied, "If you had asked before yesterday I would have granted your request, but from today I cannot do so. You see, the apostles Peter and Paul have been sent to guide my soul to heaven and they are here with me now. I see them holding a kind of cloth with marvelous gold and artwork. I must go with them to my Lord who sent them. God hears your prayers. He will give life to you. I pray God's blessing on your wives, children, and homes; I leave you my badger skin coat and my garden tools. I have no doubt that if you carry these with you when enemies attack,

God will deliver you. Do not be sad at my leaving you. For I truly believe that Christ, with whom I now go to stay, will give you whatever I ask of Him in heaven no less than when I prayed to Him on earth."[4]

Heaven's Saints Strengthen People in Life

The Hebrew Scriptures contain rich examples of God sending messengers from heaven to believers on earth, as in the account in Genesis of Abraham (Genesis 18). In the Gospels, we read that Jesus needed friends to strengthen him before his great trial (Matthew 17:1–13). He was given three earthly friends (John, Peter, and James) and two heavenly friends (Moses and Elijah).

Through the centuries, close friends of Christ in heaven have appeared to people living on earth, to strengthen them in time of need. There are, of course, the well-known apparitions of Mary, Jesus' mother. Apostles, saints, or Christians who were once acquaintances on earth appear in the dreams of many people. As our culture grows more sensitive to the Otherworld, it is almost commonplace for sensitive people to become aware of spiritual presences that leave impressions on the soul. Recently, I shared a meal in Glastonbury with a group of people, most of whom had encountered spiritual presences earlier that day. Christians will apply the test "by their fruit you shall know them" (Matthew 7:16) to such encounters.

The followers of Ignatius, the third bishop of Antioch, who was thrown to the lions in about 110 BCE, wept and slept together through the night after his death—and then suddenly, Ignatius appeared, embraced some, and prayed for others. The company was greatly strengthened by these appearances and sang many praises to God.[5]

The night before the young Northumbrian King Oswald had to confront an army three times the size of his, Columba appeared to him and promised that he would be protected and given victory. Oswald won the battle.

> To accompany other people,
> along with their loved ones,
> up to the gate of death
> is to enter Holy Ground.
> To stand in an awesome place
> where the wind
> of the Spirit blows;
> to encounter peace and grief,
> insight, intimacy and pain
> on a level not found
> in ordinary living.

> By the side of the dying
> we learn stillness,
> waiting, simply being;
> the arts of quietness
> and keeping watch,
> prayer beyond words.
>
> —PENELOPE WILCOCK[6]

Heaven's Saints Escort People at Death

When people are close to death, the curtain between this world and the next is sometimes drawn aside for a moment. They may become aware of presences coming near to them, friends or loved ones who have gone before them, or holy people who lived and died in the place where they died. An awesome energy can surround the moment of death.

A child was with Maedoc (the sixth-century bishop of Ferns, Ireland) by a large standing cross. The child saw Maedoc mount a golden ladder that reached from earth to heaven. When Maedoc came down again, the child could not look in his face because of its brilliance.

"Where did you go?" the child asked him.

This was Maedoc's reply: "I went with the gladness of the company of heaven to meet the soul of Columcille as it went to join them for he was my own in this world."

Soul Friends After Death

In the Celtic tradition death—like life—is itself a journey. The soul takes its time to leave the body, so it is important not to let the body of the dead person be unattended. There is no arbitrary cut-off point when we must cease to pray for someone who is on our hearts. Even if that person dies, we can continue to pray, because timing is not ours to command; it is God's.

Whenever Flann was about to engage in a battle, he would go to Samthann, his local abbess and friend, for prayer. On one occasion, he went to battle without first obtaining her prayers, and he was killed. On hearing of this, Samthann called her sisters to prayer, telling them, "Our friend Flann is being led by demons to painful places." She fell into an ecstasy. When she awoke, she said to the sisters, "Let's give thanks to God because the soul for whom you prayed has been taken from torment to peace through our prayers and God's immense compassion."

The lives of the Celtic saints show us that Soul Friendships are spiritual bonds that last beyond this life into eternity, for they flow directly from God, who is the pattern of all friendship, the center and source of all human relationships. In the words of Edward Sellner, "soul friendship joins friends together in a common dwelling that neither time nor space nor death itself can separate: the dwelling of the soul and of the heart."[7]

Summary

Accounts of early Irish Soul Friends give us insight into tender sharing and giving at the time of death. A good Soul Friend will help a Seeker become familiar with the angels and saints in heaven.

EXERCISES

For Soul Friends and Seekers

1. Ask yourself: what are you really afraid of? When you can name it, your fear begins to shrink. Now place this fear on an imaginary altar, which is surrounded by a heavenly company. What happens?

2. Edward Sellner described how a "Cuthbert figure" recurred in his dreams, so he began, in waking life, to hold dialogues with him about the concerns of his heart. Think of a saint with whom you strongly identify, and begin an imaginary dialogue.

For Seekers

3. Find an unhurried time when you and your Soul Friend (or another person) can talk through what you would like from your Soul Friend on your deathbed or vice versa.

Read More

Henri J. Nouwen's *Our Greatest Gift: A Meditation on Dying and Caring* (HarperOne, 2009) explores the gifts that the dying and the living can give to one another.

Penelope Wilcock's *Spiritual Care of Dying and Bereaved People* (SPCK, 1996) provides an honest look at the spiritual care of dying and bereaved people.

Maggie Callanan and Patricia Kelley's *Final Gifts: Understanding the Special Awareness, Needs, and Communications of the Dying* (Simon & Schuster, 2012) is based on two hospice nurses' experiences with patients at the end of life.

Notes

1. Robert Alexander Stewart Macalister, trans. *The Latin and Irish Lives of Ciaran* (New York, NY: Macmillan, 1921).

2. Marjory Kennedy-Fraser and Kenneth Macleod, eds. *Songs of the Hebrides and Other Celtic Songs from the Highlands of Scotland* (London, UK: Boosey, 1909).

3. John O'Donohue. *Eternal Echoes: Celtic Reflections on Our Yearning to Belong* (New York, NY: HarperCollins, 2000), p. 21.

4. Paraphrased from Alexander Boyle, trans. *St. Ninian and the Life of Monenna* (Brussels, BE: Analecta Bollandiana, 1973).

5. Ante-Nicene Fathers. *The Martyrdom of Ignatius* (Grand Rapids, MI: Eerdmans, 1981), vol. 1, p. 131.

6. Penelope Wilcock. *Spiritual Care of Dying and Bereaved People* (London, UK: SPCK, 1996), p. 24.

7. Edward Sellner. "Early Celtic Soul Friendship," *The Aisling Magazine,* issue 19, 1996, https://www.aislingmagazine.com/aislingmagazine/articles/TAM19/Friendship.html.

The Celtic Book of Days

Ancient Wisdom for Each Day of the Year from the Celtic Followers of Christ

The ancient Celts found God's presence in each ordinary moment of the day. Everything they encountered revealed to them the presence of the sacred; each day was deep with meaning. Now you too can practice the Celts' faith, as you take a few moments to immerse yourself in their wisdom. These small daily moments of reflection and insight will open your heart to each day and all it holds.

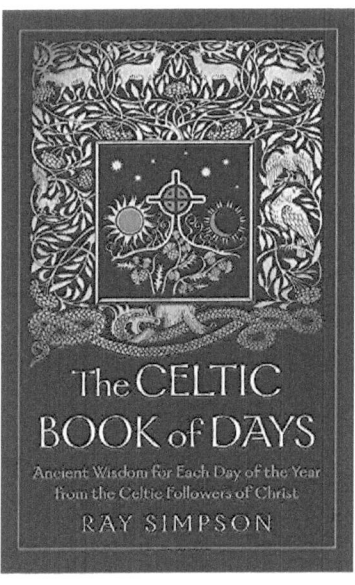

Paperback Price: $14.99

Kindle Price: $4.99

Celtic Christianity
Deep Roots for a Modern Faith

The world of the long-ago Celts appeals to many of us in the twenty-first century. Whether we are looking to find our cultural heritage or are seeking an alternative to worn and restrictive religious forms, the earth-centered, woman-friendly, inclusive faith of the Christian Celts offers us a deep-rooted alternative approach to traditional Christianity. The Celts experienced "thin places," where they sensed the supernatural world; they honored their poets, singers, and artists; and they passionately followed the Christ of the Gospels. Theirs was a church without walls, which lived naturally and comfortably within the community. Ray Simpson has spent most of his life walking in the footsteps of the Christian Celts, and now he allows us to experience for ourselves their dynamic spirituality.

Paperback Price: $14.99

Kindle Price: $4.99

Tree of Life
Celtic Prayers to the Universal Christ

Like a vast, ever-growing Tree of Life, Christ—the expression of Divine love—expands endlessly throughout the universe. This is the perspective of ancient Celtic spirituality, and it is this concept that Ray Simpson reveals in his poem-prayers. Inspired by the traditional Celtic style of prayer, he gives words to our individual relationships with God. He speaks of the wonder, beauty, and love revealed through the Universal Christ, the Tree of Life that includes all that is. Each and everything in creation is sacred, for everything is a word of God—and we too are called to be God's words to our world.

Paperback Price: $9.99

Kindle Price: $4.99

Water from an Ancient Well
Celtic Spirituality for Modern Life

Using story, scripture, reflection, and prayer, this book offers readers a taste of the living water that refreshed the ancient Celts. The author invites readers to imitate the Celtic saints who were aware of God as a living presence in everybody and everything. This ancient perspective gives radical new alternatives to modern faith practices, ones that are both challenging and constructively positive. This is a Christianity big enough to embrace the entire world.

Paperback Price: $19.99

Kindle Price: $5.99

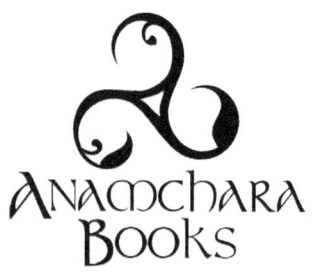

www.AnamcharaBooks.com

www.ingramcontent.com/pod-product-compliance
Lightning Source LLC
Chambersburg PA
CBHW060515080526
44586CB00012B/494